Beyon... ...histle

Frank D. Richardson.

Oct 2001

Beyond The Final Whistle

A Life of Football and Faith

John Boyers

Hodder & Stoughton
LONDON SYDNEY AUCKLAND

British Library Cataloguing in Publication Data
A record for this book is available from the British Library

ISBN 0 340 75627 6

Typeset by Avon Dataset Ltd, Bidford-on-Avon, Warks

Printed and bound in Great Britain by
Clays Ltd, St Ives plc

Hodder & Stoughton
A Division of Hodder Headline Ltd
338 Euston Road
London NW1 3BH

Contents

Foreword

It is one of those curious quirks of history that two key dates in John Boyers' remarkable life have special significance for me also. It was in 1977, as you will discover, that John first became involved as a chaplain at Watford Football Club. By sheer coincidence that was a big year for me too – the year that I commentated on my first FA Cup Final, between Liverpool and Manchester United, for the BBC – so it is with particular pleasure that I think back to the days of my earliest memories of John.

I remember visiting the Watford training ground one day and wondering what on earth was going on. Who was that bearded chap running round the track with the players? He certainly wasn't a member of the squad that I recognised. I was later introduced to the man I now consider to be a real pioneer in his field.

John was a minister at the Baptist church just a few hundred yards from the ground, and to my mind was the perfect man for the post of chaplain at Watford. The summer of 1977 was also, of course, when Graham Taylor took charge at the club and oversaw what has become one of the most extraordinary rags to riches stories of modern day football. Throughout their dramatic rise from the bottom to the top of the Football League, an ascent which reached its peak when Watford themselves appeared at Wembley in the FA Cup Final, the club never forgot its roots in the local community. The family atmosphere at Watford has always impressed me and I believe John, with his down-to-earth, honest and affable character, personified it.

The second date of great significance to us both is 1992, the year that John and his family felt the call to move to Manchester. Here the interesting parallel with my own life continues because 1992 saw the return to our screens of *Match of the Day*, after an absence of seven years. For millions of football fans in England the year will be remembered for the birth of the Premiership, the dawn of a new age for the sport in this country. But perhaps those with the fondest memories of that year will be the fans of Manchester United. Eric Cantona joined the club from championship holders Leeds, and that season the Red Devils won the league for the first time since 1967. The rest, as they say, is history.

John has continued his ground breaking work in sports chaplaincy at Old Trafford, and his efforts, combined with those of several excellent chaplains working at a few other clubs, have raised the appreciation of the position from within the game to new heights. I believe the years since the start of the Premiership have been the hardest possible time for football chaplaincy to make an impact. The game has never been as high-profile, money-minded or, for want of a better word, 'secular' than it is now. There are economic forces that by their nature are pulling the game away from the person-centred, selfless and spiritual values that John and others are striving to promote.

John has always taken his job as seriously as anyone I know, and this has enabled him to break new ground. The charity that he directs, SCORE, has helped establish a nationwide network of sports chaplains, and not just in professional football. Of particular note is the organisation's recent placing of the very first chaplain in the world of horse-racing – a sport that to some people's minds could not be further removed from the Church!

I believe the secret of John's success is his character. There are many in the world of football who would be wary of anyone openly proclaiming themselves to be an evangelical Christian; who would resent a preacher coming down from the pulpit to force his beliefs upon them. But such an over-bearing style is alien to John's nature. He is compassionate without ever being intrusive, caring without ever going over the top. And that is why he is held in such esteem at Watford, Manchester United and beyond.

John Motson

Preface

Beyond the Final Whistle has been written because I was asked by Hodder Headline, and by several Christian people, to share some of my experiences as a chaplain in the world of sport. This book is not an exposé, telling the private and intimate details of the lives of the stars. Indeed, I want to make it clear that the chaplain must deal absolutely confidentially with those with whom he interacts. So, the idea of recounting personal and private conversations is beyond this chaplain's intentions.

I do want to explain how, as just an ordinary young lad, I grew up with an interest in sport and how God got involved with that young life. This is a story of football and a faith. It tries to intertwine the two. I hope, in places, it's amusing, informative, and perhaps, too, a little instructive about Christian life and faith.

This preface gives me the opportunity to express some thanks. I want to thank all those who have allowed me, and, indeed, other chaplains into their private sports worlds as we seek to serve them with discretion, integrity, availability and appropriateness. Particularly, I would thank all of those who, since 1977 at Watford, and then from September 1992 at Manchester United, have allowed me access to function as the official chaplain at their football club, and indeed for the support and affirmation that they have given to the chaplain's role.

It is also necessary to express thanks to those whose vision and support was so important to the establishment of SCORE in 1991, and its subsequent development. Many Christian leaders showed vision and commitment, and many people from a wide range of churches throughout the country have been faithful in their prayers and support for SCORE. All of you deserve our thanks.

I would particularly like to think Lynne Brumpton for her devoted work in preparing the manuscripts to submit to Hodder Headline, and to David Moloney for his help and encouragement on behalf of the company.

However, supremely, I want to express my thanks to my family – to Anne, my wife, and Andrew John and Jonathan James, my sons. They are a wonderful family! I appreciate Anne's friendship and support since our marriage in 1972, and the willingness, in more recent years, of the boys to accommodate their father's full and varied lifestyle which often has taken me away from home. In normal local church ministry and now in this very specialised work in the world of sport, my family have been a great resource and a tremendous support, and I express my thanks to them here and now.

I write as the chaplain at Manchester United Football Club, but Old Trafford is not where my story starts. I hope you will read on and see how this adventure with football and faith all kicked off, how it has progressed, and how my work with Manchester United Football Club fits into the wider context of my work as the National Director of SCORE.

1

'Up the Mariners'

Blundell Park, Cleethorpes, the traditional home of Grimsby Town Football Club, was where my love for football was nurtured. I have many memories of that place, some ecstatically happy, some desperately sad, and some just typical football tales.

I remember one occasion when Swansea was the visiting team and their supporters, crowded into one end of the ground, at half-time were chanting 'Wales, Wales, Wales'. The Grimsby supporters in another stand responded to Swansea's patriotic fervour with a chant of 'Dolphins, Dolphins, Dolphins'. I thought that was brilliant, and it's a pity that that sort of banter isn't heard more at football grounds these days. I remember as a young teacher in Grimsby walking onto the pitch at the end of a night of celebration when Laurie McMenemy had taken the team to promotion from Division Four into Division Three. I think the attendance that night against Exeter City was about 22,000, and the sense of joy, jubilation and perhaps relief that at last Grimsby Town had found success was something that only football fans would really appreciate.

I remember, too, the hard times and the sad times. In the 1960s we drew 2–2 at home with Sunderland, but while they went up to the then First Division, we dropped down from the Second to the Third on a goal average that was 0.008 of a goal. I think our nearest rival drew 0–0 and stayed up. Had the results been reversed, with Grimsby drawing 0–0 and our nearest rival drawing 2–2, they would have gone down. There was great sadness and despair on that occasion. On a hideously cold, unpleasant and wet east-coast winter Saturday, when Grimsby played Gillingham, I remember walking to the game in torrential rain and watching a 0–0 draw in almost unplayable conditions. I returned home chilled to the marrow, pretty well saturated, with my incredulous father wondering why this devotion to Grimsby Town Football Club. I remember Dad asking: 'Were there men with white coats as you went in?' It was only later that I realised this was a reference to the white-coated nurses who used to care for the inmates at the lunatic asylum just outside Lincoln, but all football fans are familiar with such stories of emotion and dedication.

Blundell Park wasn't, though, the absolute beginning of my love for football. My first recollections of seeing the game are on television. In 1953, just before the Coronation, Mum and Dad had bought a television. There weren't many about then, but we had bought one. I remember it being a 'Cossor', with a twelve-inch screen. This amazing piece of technological equipment enabled the Boyers family and many of their relations to watch the Coronation that summer, and also made it possible for me to become familiar with programmes like

Muffin the Mule, Andy Pandy, The Flower Pot Men – and also football. I can remember my uncles gathering one Saturday in May to watch the Cup Final. My behaviour must have disturbed them a little bit, because someone suggested I be taken outside to play in the garden for a while. But I soon began to appreciate what this little black and white box in the corner had to offer – including the game of football. I recall images of grey little players drifting around grey stadia scoring grey goals while huge crowds of grey flat-capped men waved their rattles, cheered and threw hats in the air. At least the black and white of Newcastle must have looked good on those televisions in 1955. One of my clearest memories is probably the 1960 final when Wolverhampton Wanderers beat Blackburn 3–0. I remember little Norman Deeley playing on the right wing, and scoring, I think, two goals.

By that time I had been to see my first football match at Blundell Park, Cleethorpes. I recall my father taking me into the little turnstile, explaining to the man who took the money that this was my first ever game, and asking if it would be possible for him to lift me over the turnstile while Dad paid for his place on the terraces. The man willingly agreed. As I walked round the back of the stand onto the terraces, holding my dad's hand, I was amazed at the number of supporters who were there to watch Grimsby Town. I also remember being absolutely overwhelmed at the size of the players. I recall thinking, these are real people, they are actually 'man-sized' people. That may seem a strange comment, but the only football that I had seen up until then was on our twelve-inch television screen. It suddenly dawned on me that this was actual reality – the little figures that I had seen on our 'Cosser' television set actually represented real people!'

I quite enjoyed my first experience of football at Blundell Park, and my dad periodically would take me to games. I continued to enjoy the excitement and atmosphere of watching Grimsby Town. I remember towards the start of one particular season Dad took me to my first ever night match. We were playing Swindon Town, who had just got promoted from the Third Division to the Second, and it was probably the first night match of that season. I think Grimsby lost 2–0. We arrived late with about ten or twelve minutes already gone, and Grimsby, by that time, were already trailing 1 or 2–0 to a very young Swindon side that was full of talented and speedy players. I think Don Rogers and Mike Summerbee were amongst their team on that occasion. However, a lad of my age was not aware of up-and-coming starlets. I was only aware of a team wearing red who had beaten my beloved team in black and white stripes.

In the early sixties, I was eventually allowed to go to Blundell Park on my own. That first time I followed the same routine that Dad and I always used, going through the same turnstile and standing in the same sort of area in the Osmond Stand. I was still trying to understand the right way to behave at football matches and observed the people around me, imitating what they did. I cheered when they cheered and shouted 'Come on the Town' when they shouted. When one of the players went down injured, I noticed that people around me cheered and shouted, 'Get him off, referee, he's rubbish', and similar helpful comments. I decided, therefore, that that's what you did when someone went down injured. It wasn't long before another player went down injured, and, amid the hushed quiet around our corner of Blundell Park, a trainer ran onto the pitch. My squeaky, youthful little voice broke

4

the silence, 'He's rubbish, get him off! Referee, take him off, he's useless.' To my great embarrassment no sooner had the words left my lips than I felt hundreds of eyes focusing on me. One man said, 'He's not useless at all lad, he's *our* best player.' I suddenly realised that the cries and taunts of derision were focused on *their* injured player when he went down, and the reaction to *our* injured players when they went down was quite, quite different. I learned from that situation, and decided it was better to keep quiet and watch the game of football, rather than try and emulate the shouting and chanting of those around me. Perhaps that was a very good lesson to learn in the early stages of my support for the Mariners.

As I grew up into my teenage years, life at Blundell Park, Cleethorpes was not too dissimilar from the rollercoaster that we called 'the dip in the dips' at Wonderland, Cleethorpes – one of the exciting attractions of Cleethorpes North Promenade. In short, it was full of ups and downs. The ups included a time in the 1960s when some excellent football was played under the management of Jimmy McGuigan. At left back the team included Graham Taylor, who was later to become a very successful club manager and manager of England. It also included the thin frail Scotsman, Matt Tees, who had been signed from Airdrie and who was to become a hero and a legend in Grimsby. I remember on one occasion going to watch Grimsby play Scunthorpe United, one of our local rivals. The game had been hyped up because two young stars were in the Scunthorpe side. One was a goalkeeper called Ray Clemence, who used to sell deck chairs on Skegness seafront in his summer holidays. The other was a talented young right winger called Keegan. Grimsby beat that side 7–1, and I think our left winger, Brian Hill, scored three and

Matt Tees also scored three, with his striking partner, Rod Green, scoring the other goal for Grimsby. I went home thinking that Clemence and Keegan were overrated and probably had no serious future in the game. Fortunately, coaches know more about football than most fans on the terraces!

The late 1960s and early 1970s saw me less at Blundell Park. I went to Nottingham to the Teacher Training College at Clifton. When the issue of my future was raised by careers teachers at school, although a somewhat shy teenager, I was always pretty sure that I wanted to teach geography. Perhaps I might have gone to Nottingham University to do a geography degree and follow that with a postgraduate teaching certificate, but I was advised to consider the new Education degree that was being promoted at Nottingham College of Education at Clifton. I enrolled for the Batchelor of Education degree studying geography and education.

I generally enjoyed my time at Nottingham and it was of lasting significance to me for two reasons. Not only was it where I trained for my first major profession in life, teaching, but it was there that I found two, lasting and significant relationships. The first was my relationship with my wife. Anne and I were both students at Clifton. We became friends there, were engaged just before Anne left in 1970, and married in 1972.

The second relationship was a spiritual one. I had always had a sense that there was a God. I had been brought up in a northern, non-conformist home. Mum and Dad were very involved in the local Methodist church, as, it seemed, were most of the family. Father was the Church Society steward, Aunt Joan looked after the primary Sunday school, Uncle

Wilf looked after the junior Sunday school, Aunt Margaret frequently played the organ for services. Whenever we could, my mother, father, sister and I would attend church on a Sunday. Our home was quite focused on church and faith, with a Christian outlook and teaching. From the age of four or five to fourteen or fifteen I went through primary, junior and senior Sunday school and throughout that time I never doubted the existence of God. The idea that there was a God who was responsible for the creation and sustaining of this world, and who exercised his authority over us in some way seemed reasonable and logical to me. But, in truth, some of my faith was a little bit superstitious.

One Saturday lunchtime I bargained with God. My beloved Grimsby Town had lost their last four matches, all without scoring a goal, and as I watched *Grandstand* that Saturday lunchtime I remember thinking that maybe they really needed some divine help and inspiration. I sort of prayed a semi-prayer that said something like, 'If you help Grimsby win today, God, I'll really try hard in Sunday school tomorrow.' Grimsby did win and I did try hard, but whether God was involved or not is a matter for debate. That was the kind of faith that I had during my early college days in Nottingham: God is there and we must appease him. It was the kind of faith many people have, which tends to call on God to do remarkable things in extreme emergencies. Yet, while I was at Nottingham I met people whose faith was quite different.

I used to go to the local Methodist church at least once a Sunday, and I guess many of my fellow students would have regarded me as a fairly religious, fairly devout Christian individual. However, I met up with people from the Christian Union, and they were different. They knew I went to church regularly and invited me to go to their Bible study. 'What do you do in a Bible study?' I asked.

'Ah, we study the Bible,' they said.

'Why?'

'Oh, we try and learn from it; we try and understand how God wants to speak to us, help us and instruct us today.'

Now I could have done with some help and instruction with aspects of my geography course, but I wasn't too keen to do extra Bible study, so I declined that option. About a month later members of the Christian Union invited me to something else. 'Do you want to come to our prayer meeting?' they suggested.

'What do you do in a prayer meeting?' I asked.

'We pray,' was their reply.

'Why?' I questioned. 'Is somebody ill? Is there some grave crisis? What do we need to pray about? Is it exam time? Is someone going into hospital?' You see, my experience of praying was that if there was an utter emergency that really needed God's help and intervention then I tended to call on him, but that was about all. So, the idea of praying, particularly if there were no apparent reasons to pray, seemed a little over-enthusiastic from my point of view. I decided not to go to the prayer meeting.

Two to three months later I received my third, and perhaps most significant, invitation. 'Do you want to come to the Pizza Party we're holding?' they said. Now that really did interest me. I wasn't terribly turned on by the thought of a Bible study or a prayer meeting, but a 'Pizza Party' sounded interesting. Attracted by the idea of food, drink and some new people to meet I decided I would go along. I got to know the people from the Christian Union. They were interesting people who were pleasant and genuine. They seemed concerned, trustworthy and honest, but most of all they were people who were quite open about speaking of their faith in God, and this faith in God was a bit different from mine.

I wasn't *sure* if God existed, but I *believed* he did, and that was the sum total of my faith. For them it was different; it was as though they knew God existed. They didn't just believe and hope, they *knew* God existed. What is more, God seemed to exist within their lives; he seemed to be 'part of them'. They were really serious followers. Believing in God wasn't just believing in his existence: believing in God was giving their lives to follow him. They wanted to do what he wanted. They sought to put into practice the teaching of Christ and the New Testament. It was quite an interesting experience. These were seriously religious people, it seemed.

I began to talk to members of the Christian Union about what they believed and why they believed it. Although they came from many different backgrounds, all had the same basic message to tell. They all spoke of a place, a time, or a period when they began to become very personally aware of the power and the presence of God in their lives. I was familiar with talking, singing and thinking about God, particularly in a church service, but this whole concept of God breaking into our lives, dealing with what was wrong, and making us new, of coming to live within us, putting his life, love, truth and strength, his presence and his power within our lives – that was quite different for me. What is more I found that there were people from many different church backgrounds who were telling a similar story about their real faith in Jesus Christ. There were people who worshipped in Anglican,

Baptist, Methodist, or Pentecostal churches. I remember talking to one girl with a very vibrant, real and personal faith who worshipped at a Roman Catholic church. Another girl in the Christian Union said she was one of the Christian Brethren, and I remember commenting that I thought she looked female. She said that you did not have to be male to be one of the Christian Brethren. I looked at her with an amazingly puzzled look and said, 'Well, I'm a Methodist.' So far that had been my answer for everything in my Christian life. Now people were starting to talk to me and ask me questions: 'How did I become a Christian?' 'When did I become a Christian?' My answer was still the same: 'Well, I'm a Methodist.'

I began to realise that my affiliation with a denomination, my association with a particular church, was a long way from the experience of those who belonged to the Christian Union. For them the church mattered, but it did not matter as much as their coming to know the reality of God in Jesus Christ. That really set me thinking. I began to read little booklets about the Christian faith and about how an individual can become a Christian. One tiny booklet, written by an Anglican minister, John Stott, called *Becoming a Christian*, was very helpful to me. I came to realise that, although I was a churchgoer with a sense of God's existence, I had not been touched by the truth of the message of Jesus Christ. I had not been transformed by the person of Jesus Christ and the power of the story about his death and resurrection. Let me give you an illustration that will parallel the situation I found myself in.

A dramatic air–sea rescue takes place close to some rugged cliffs on the coast of England. During a horrendous storm a small coaster loses the power in its engines and is forced by the wind and waves towards the treacherous cliffs. It sends out a Mayday signal and an RAF helicopter is scrambled. Ploughing its way through the wind and the rain, eventually it hovers over the boat while a winchman is sent down, and, one by one, the small crew is rescued. The next day people read about that rescue in their newspapers, and are inspired at the bravery of the helicopter crew and are thankful for the safe outcome of the rescue. However, there are others whose thankfulness and admiration is even stronger. The staff of the coastguard station, situated at the top of the cliffs were the first to become aware of the plight of the boat. It was they who made contact with the RAF air-sea rescue team, and it was they who were watching and monitoring the whole rescue operation. They saw it all happen and they actually visited the rescued crew in hospital. They spoke with the media. They recounted the whole story. Yet, great though their thanks and appreciation is, it does not equate in any way with the thankfulness and the appreciation of the crew who were winched up from the boat into the rescue helicopter. They had been about to drown as their boat was crushed on the rocks. There had been no way out, and then, suddenly, the helicopter appeared, the winchman came down and held out a hand of safety and of rescue. Each of those men was able to speak from personal experience of how they had been saved from the gales and the waves on that day. The public might read about it in a newspaper and be inspired by the facts, and the coastguards might have monitored it and been thankful for all that they had observed, but it was the crew themselves who had personally experienced the whole of the rescue operation. It wasn't just a story for the crew: it was a real experience.

My coming to Christian faith parallels that little story. The people I met in the Christian Union in Nottingham were able to talk to me about how God had rescued them spiritually. It was real and it was personal. They also pointed out to me the worth, but actual inadequacy, of my present Christian experience. I knew a lot of the Christian story, I'd moved around in very Christian circles, and I knew a lot of people who, quite clearly, had come to experience a life-changing relationship with Jesus Christ, but that relationship was something I had not yet established. I had never responded to the issues raised by the basic Christian message, the gospel. Indeed, my thinking made it hard for me to really see the relevance of the gospel. I viewed myself as a pretty decent individual who tried to live a reasonably helpful and kind life, and I thought God was quite fortunate to have me rooting for him. However, the truth is that, however hard we try and however good we seem to be, not one of us is perfect, and therefore we need to be forgiven. Therefore the message of God's forgiveness through Jesus is relevant to all of us. It was that understanding that helped me to commit my life to God, to receive his forgiveness and to live for Jesus. However, that experience, which was very personal and life changing, did not cause me to become a monk or a hermit. I felt new, I felt forgiven, and I felt strengthened. I had a new friendship with God. I felt spiritually alive. With a new sense of peace and a sense of purpose came the conviction that I was in the right place, that God wanted me to train to be a teacher. I continued my involvement with the Christian Union throughout my remaining years at college. It was in the Christian Union that I met Anne, the lady who was to become my fiancée in 1970, and my wife in August 1972. (On that day Grimsby drew

1–1 with York City in their first match of the season. Matt Tees scored Grimsby's goal.) A memorable day!

After I finished my student days at Nottingham, I returned to Grimsby to begin teaching geography at Cleethorpes Boys Grammar School. Founded in 1823, it was a wonderful establishment called 'Clee Boys'. The ethos and most of the staff of the school seemed quite original. I remember dearly the headmaster who interviewed me for my job. His two key questions were: 'My Boyers, if we appointed you to this school, would you wear a gown while you were teaching? I think it's very important.' Clearly, I was required to answer 'yes' to that question. I did so. Then came the second question: 'Mr Boyers, do you play cricket?'

'Yes I do,' I said.

'Are you a batsman or a bowler?'

'I do a little bit of both.'

'Ah, an all-rounder! if we appointed you to this geography job, would you play in the staff cricket team?'

'I'd be delighted to, Mr Shaw.'

'The job's yours, Mr Boyers,' the Head announced, and so I got my first teaching job on the basis of wearing a gown and playing cricket, but not both at the same time, of course.

There were many happy memories from Clee Boys and an abundance of amusing incidents the like of which, were they to appear in a film or in a work of fiction, would be deemed too far-fetched to be believable. Such an incident was my first Founders Day Service.

Every year the school marched from its buildings on Clee Road, Cleethorpes, down to the parish church of Old Clee, maybe half a mile away, where some 550 boys squeezed into pews and were treated to a Founders Day Service.

My first experience of this occasion happened to coincide with a new vicar gracing the Founders Day pulpit. There was a tradition amongst the staff, that when the speaker stood up to give the address on Founders Day, one of the PE staff would time the whole of the sermon with a stopwatch. The clock was stopped as soon as the speaker finished his presentation, either by a definite 'amen', a 'we'll now sing the hymn', or by sitting down. The entire staff were invited to have a sweepstake on the length of the sermon. It was usually between twenty and thirty minutes, so a lot of pounds were laid on 22 minutes or 24 minutes or 26 minutes 38 seconds, or whatever. Some went to extremes – 42 minutes, 17 minutes, and even 13 minutes. There was a furore over my first Founders Day Service. The new vicar, having stood up and surveyed the children in his church, began with words that I still remember: 'Wet day' – there was a long pause – 'cold church' – a longer pause – 'bored children . . . You don't particularly want to listen to me, and I know very little about you and the significance of this occasion. I am new to the parish, but your teachers know about this school. Your teachers like boys with enquiring minds, and I am asking you to enquire. Go back to the classrooms, say to your teachers – why do we have Founders Day? Who did found the school? Why do we have these services? What is the significance of us remembering the history of this school?' There were a few other words and phrases as what appeared to be an introduction rapidly took on the tone of a conclusion, a summing up. We were astonished when the vicar sat down. A 'click' was heard as Mike Hetherington stopped the stopwatch and, when the staff were eventually reassembled in the staff room at lunchtime, the announcement was put on the board: 3 minutes

28 seconds. The nearest guess was more than ten minutes away. No one could believe that the Founders Day Service had contained such a remarkably short address. Many were happy at the length of the address, but not happy that one member of staff who had guessed 14 minutes 29 seconds actually won the Founders Day sweepstake. Happy memories of an old school with old traditions.

Another of the school's traditions was Morning Assembly. The Head would mount the rostrum, gown billowing after him, mortar board tucked under his arm, put down his books and papers, and look at the school. The boys stilled themselves. He would look at his notes, and then look up again before he addressed them with a 'Thought for the Day'. This was our daily routine. The staff were assembled behind him on wooden chairs, on the back of an old wooden stage. I remember vividly one morning when the Head came in, mounted the stage, placed his papers and notes as usual, looked at the school, checked on his notes, and then raised his eyes again to present 'Thought for the Day'. As he did so he noticed a small urchin of a First Year acting somewhat indiscreetly with his nasal cavity, and sought to reprimand him. The scenario sounded like this to the teachers seated behind: 'Thought for the Day' – slight pause – 'stop picking your nose'. I was sitting next to Alf, who taught Latin. He turned to me, tapped me on the shoulder, and said, 'Is that Old Testament or New?' It was that sort of school, that sort of staff. Awesomely happy memories of incredible situations.

After two and a bit years of teaching at Clee Grammar I moved on to the Wintringham School in Grimsby. That had been my old grammar school, but it was changing rapidly. Two or three years earlier it had become co-educational, having joined with the girls' grammar school, and it was now about to become comprehensive. Over the next four or five years it was to change from a 1000 pupil school to an 1800 pupil school. Staff changes were being made and I took on the post of second in the geography department. By this time Anne and I were married and living in Grimsby. She was teaching at a local primary school, and I was now teaching at a local secondary school. We were very settled in terms of our professional involvements, the house where we were living and our involvement in a local church.

I had begun to do some preaching on the local Methodist circuit, and Anne and I were involved in leading the senior Sunday school and a Friday night youth meeting. I was still a devoted Grimsby Town fan, but instead of watching them regularly on Saturdays, I was actually playing a bit of football myself – in fact Saturday was becoming quite a sporty day. In the mornings I usually found myself coaching or refereeing one of the school teams, and then in the afternoon playing for Torino. This does not mean I was flown out to Italy to guest for one of the premier teams in Turin. Torino play in the Fourth Division of the Grimsby Saturday League, and in the summer of 1973 or 1974 were looking for new players. I had gone down and joined in training, and they seemed a reasonable bunch of chaps, so I signed on and played for Torino. I don't like to tell people that this was Grimsby Saturday League Division Four, but that is the truth, and truth is important.

It was good fun without a great deal of success. We did, however, feature one week in the *Grimsby Saturday Football Telegraph*. It was about a month after we'd bought a new set of kit. Although it didn't make us play any better, we did look very smart. The local press photographer saw this remarkably smart team on the playing fields before kick-off, and asked us to group together so that he could take our photograph. It was only afterwards that he enquired about our record – played 13, won 2, drawn 4, lost 7. He put a very nice piece in with the photographs, which went something like: 'One of the smartest looking outfits in Grimsby Saturday League Division Four is Torino. Although they don't have much success with their playing, they are a really nice bunch of chaps, and their kit is one of the best in the division.' That was the nicest compliment we probably got that season, and for one or two others as well.

A year or two later a huge change took place. We were settled in a nice house. We were enjoying jobs in pleasant schools, and professionally the way ahead seemed mapped out for us. Yet gradually, over a period of months, we began to feel that God was challenging us to leave teaching and to train for Christian ministry. It is hard to explain to people, who may not understand, how it happened. It was not a bright light 'Damascus Road' type of experience. As preachers said things in sermons, as I read books, as we read the Bible as part of our normal Christian devotional reading, as friends and others spoke to us in our day-to-day lives God seemed to be speaking to us. In many and in varied ways we had a growing sense that God wanted us to leave our work in Grimsby so that I could train for Christian ministry, and that is what we decided to do in the summer of 1976. We told parents, friends and colleagues, and, in late August 1976, headed with a car stacked full of 'necessaries' to the south of England and our new home, Watford.

2

Elton John's Taylor-made Army

Anne and I knew very little about Northwood, or North-west London, when we moved down from Grimsby in 1976. I think our first visit to an estate agent was in Rickmansworth. The estate agent looked at us quizzically as I explained we were moving down from the North and were hoping to buy a house in this sort of area. 'What, precisely, are you looking for?' he enquired. I described what we had in Grimsby, and the sort of price we might get for it, suggesting we might be looking for a three-bedroomed house with front and rear garden, central heating and a garage for around £10,000. The man stared at me with an amazed look on his face, and then smiled and said: 'We could probably get you a garage for £10,000.' We came to realise that the price of property, in Northwood particularly, and even in Rickmansworth and the surrounding area, was considerably more than we were used to in Grimsby.

We eventually settled in Watford. Anne got a teaching job

in a primary school in North Watford, and, after a few months in rented accommodation having sold our house in Grimsby, we were able to buy a maisonette. During those early months in the autumn of 1976, not only did Anne get established in her teaching job while I settled into my work at London Bible College, but together we found a new church, St James Road Baptist Church in West Watford. We got on well with the minister and his wife, Richard and Shirley Harbour, who made us very welcome. We enjoyed their style of ministry, and it was not long before Richard was suggesting that it might be possible for me to work as a student Assistant Minister for the last two years of my course at London Bible College. The college encouraged its students to have a practical, pastoral expression of Christian work and ministry. Some people went on various kinds of teams to be involved in a whole host of different activities, but we were very taken with the possibility of working with St James Road Baptist Church, and in the summer of the following year, 1977, I was officially endorsed as the Student Assistant Minister for my last two years at London Bible College.

There was another interesting development in West Watford that summer. Another northerner came to Watford. A bright young manager, Graham Taylor, left Lincoln City to take over the reins at Watford Football Club, just down the road from the church. Just a few years earlier, Elton John had become a member of the Board of the club, and a little more recently, had taken over the chairman's role. He was very keen to appoint a dynamic young manager who could take the club places, and Graham Taylor, with three excellent seasons at Lincoln City to his credit, seemed to fit the bill. After a shaky start he had stabilised the club and taken it from the Fourth to the Third Division, and in the previous season he had taken them close to the top of Division Three. The media had earmarked him as a manager who was going places. Evidently there had been various offers for his services, notably from West Bromwich Albion, but Graham had been really inspired by Elton John's drive, vision and hopes for the club at Watford.

However, despite Graham's involvement with Watford Football Club, I took very little notice of the Hornets. Deep down I was still a Grimsby Town fan, and on Saturdays preferred to play local league or Hertfordshire League football than watch Watford Football Club. In the autumn of 1977 three events occurred that really changed my attitude to Watford FC.

The first was in September when a man called Mike Pusey visited the church to talk to our housegroup leaders. As a church, we had groups which met in homes to study the Bible, pray, worship God and to be an encouragement to each other together. These were led by lay members of the church, and once a month Richard Harbour and I would gather together the housegroup leaders to try to encourage them and teach them how to be more effective in their job. Usually Richard led those meetings; I sometimes led part of them, and occasionally we brought in outside speakers. Mike Pusey, one of Richard's friends, was then at Farnborough Baptist Church. In a coffee break in the middle of that meeting, Mike came up to me and said: 'Isn't the church near Watford Football Club?' I said: 'Yes, it's very close, but they don't trouble us at all.' Mike smiled and responded: 'Have you ever thought of being involved with them? I'm chaplain at Aldershot Football Club.' This statement was followed by a long and embarrassed silence. I remember thinking, how can you believe in an all-loving and all-powerful God and still be chaplain at Aldershot Football Club? It seemed like a bit of a prison sentence to me, and I made a remark along those lines to Mike, perhaps even mentioning the word purgatory. Mike, however, was determined to convince me that there was a real job to be done. 'Chaplaincy at Aldershot, you know, is not about free tickets for games. There are people at the club who have got no link at all with the church. They don't know who the priest, minister or pastor is. When there are problems or difficulties many of them don't know who to turn to. Being a chaplain is a real job, getting alongside people, helping them, and being available to them when they meet times of need or crisis. As well as helping them, it helps me.' Mike continued. 'As a minister it is very easy to be so often surrounded by religious people that you begin to lose contact with the real world outside the church. My work with Aldershot has introduced me to the problems, pains and difficulties, questions and issues that face normal, ordinary people. It is a really worthwhile involvement, and you ought to consider it at Watford. The club is just down the road from the church. Think about being chaplain at Watford Football Club.' Our conversation ended and I told Mike that I would think about it. We finished our coffee and got on with the second half of our meeting, and, if truth be told, I didn't really think about chaplaincy at Watford Football Club for another five or six weeks.

At the autumn half-term the church had decided to put on a coffee bar for the kids in the immediate community. Coffee bars are not as popular nowadays, but in the late 1970s it was an accepted means of contacting the teenagers of the locality. We got hold of a big net from HMS *Warrior*, the NATO base in Northwood, filled it with bacofoil, shone bright coloured lights down on it and transformed the church hall to try and make it a bit more atmospheric. We built a stage at one end, and on the Monday of the week, I think, a Christian rock band came and played for us and shared about why their faith was so important to them. On the Tuesday there was a drama group, and on the Wednesday Alan West, a professional footballer for some seven or eight years who was then captain of Luton Town, came to speak. Alan used to play for Burnley and, a couple of years after his transfer some four years earlier, had become a Christian. He was going to talk about faith and football. I met him when he arrived at the church and took him down to the church hall where we chatted about the evening. In the middle of a coffee break, after he had finished talking to some of the kids who were there, we found a quiet corner and chatted about his life as captain of Luton Town. Interestingly, he too had noticed how close the church building was to Watford Football Club. 'Your church is very close to Watford Football Club,' he said. 'Have you ever thought about being chaplain there?'

'No, not really,' I replied. 'Well, only once, I had the idea thrown across me some six weeks ago.'

'Did you do anything about it?' asked Alan.

'No, not really,' I replied. 'There is a lot to do here.'

I really didn't feel 'grabbed' by the idea of getting involved with Watford Football Club. I wasn't sure about the relevance of a chaplaincy, and I wasn't sure what a chaplain would do or how he could help people. Alan then told me a story. Evidently, one of the players at his club, that very weekend, had learned that his father, who he knew was very ill, was actually terminally ill. This player, on the Monday when he came into the club, had sought out Alan West because he knew that he was a Christian. He knew that Alan's faith in Jesus Christ had really changed his life. He knew that God was very real, and very important, to Alan, and because of that, this player, faced with tragedy, had sought him out for help and comfort. He had asked Alan to pray for him, for his father and for the situation over the next two or three months, because he just didn't know how he would cope with all the pressure. 'Wouldn't it be great,' Alan said to me, 'if we had chaplains within clubs, who could help people facing those sort of difficulties? Wouldn't it be an asset if there were ministers, like you, who were involved in our football clubs, offering their support, care, and counselling expertise to those who might need it? So many people today don't have any contact with church, but when illness, death, disease, hospitalisation or family problems come they often need someone to talk to. They often need someone who will pray with them and for them. I think there is a real job for chaplains in football clubs, and I really would encourage you to get involved with Watford, and ask them if you can talk to them about chaplaincy work.' Those words from Alan West were more than just words from someone whom I had got to know. It was as though God was speaking to me.

Mike Pusey had come six weeks earlier and introduced the idea; now Alan was making the same suggestion, and I really felt that God was prompting me to get involved with Watford Football Club. I began to pray, 'Lord, are you really saying something to me? If you are, make it clear, because this is something new and different, and I do need to know that you are in it if it is to open up.' I prayed like that on the Thursday and the Friday. That same Friday evening I bought a copy of our local newspaper, *The Watford Observer*. It was free on Tuesdays and the big weekend edition, which cost 10p, was always packed with adverts, news, information and, not least, news about local sport, with some good perceptive articles by Oliver Philips over the back three or four pages. That weekend there was an interview with Graham Taylor, and I read, at first with interest and then with amazement, the Manager's words about his hopes for the football club. He wanted the club to be part of the community. He wanted to take his players into schools, factories and hospitals, to make Watford Football Club not just a football club in Watford but a football club belonging to the town and area and people of Watford. He was also quoted as saying he wanted the community to be involved with the football club on a day-to-day, week-to-week basis and wanted to find points of common interest between the community and the club.

I read those comments again with great interest. Graham seemed to be saying that he was open to members of the local community being involved with Watford Football Club. I really did feel God was saying something. I shared this feeling with Richard Harbour and we agreed to pray about the idea, before discussing it together at length at a later date. When we eventually met some three weeks later Richard had come to the conclusion that God was challenging us to become involved with Watford Football Club. I had a similar conviction. Together we agreed to write a letter to Graham Taylor, the manager at Watford Football Club, to ask if we could speak to him about the whole subject of football club chaplaincy. It wasn't long before we had a reply, and Graham gave us a date and time when we could see him in his office. I remember Richard and I leaving the church offices, turning left, walking down Vicarage Road, past the little corner shops and food outlets, turning down a side road called Occupation Road, opposite the Red Lion pub that stood on the corner, to make our way to Watford Football Club's Reception, and to Graham Taylor's office.

Graham welcomed us warmly, then took us into what looked a fairly old, dilapidated and dingy office, where he invited us to sit down. He offered us tea or coffee and, as that was brought to us, he made us feel welcomed and 'at home'. I remember Graham apologising for the state of the furniture. 'They're not the newest of chairs,' he said, 'but sorting out the furniture is the least of my problems here' – he was in the process of trying to lift the club into the upper reaches of the league. The conversation then turned to his hopes for Watford Football Club, and why we were expressing an interest in chaplaincy. He posed the question: 'Why should a club have a chaplain? What would a chaplain do?' Richard and I looked at each other, and Richard intimated that I might like to take that question. I thought: 'Thank you very much, Richard!'

I talked about the scenarios that Alan and Mike had spoken to us about. 'There are many situations where people might find chaplains helpful, Mr Taylor,' I said. 'People face all sorts of problems and difficulties: it might be young players feeling lonely and homesick because they are away from home, family and friends for the first time. It might be older established players facing frustration through long-term injury, or feeling very concerned about significant surgery that they have to undergo. It might be players who are worried because they are coming towards the end of their careers, and are not sure what they would do after football. There are also the normal ordinary everyday problems that affect players and the rest of the people who are associated with a football club. People face bereavement, personal problems, financial difficulties and the general pressure of life. Sometimes they need a bit of spiritual support and help. They might need someone to officiate at a wedding or a funeral. They might need someone to talk to, whom they can trust totally to be absolutely confidential. They might need to get a different angle on a particular situation that is troubling them. There are many opportunities for the chaplain to be available, and to have input into the lives of people.'

'Do you think the chaplain is a Bible basher?' Graham asked.

I sought to reassure him that we weren't coming in to force our message onto people who didn't want to hear, although I remember saying that, if people asked us questions about God, faith and spiritual issues, then we had the right to reply, and Graham agreed with that.

Graham had certainly come to understand something of the role of the chaplain, and in our conversation had clearly detected my accent, because after we had finished talking about the work and relevance of chaplaincy he made the comment: 'You're not really a Watford lad, are you?'

'No, no. I'm from Grimsby,' I said.

'I thought I detected a Lincolnshire accent,' said Graham. 'I was brought up in Scunthorpe, you know, and I used to play for Grimsby Town.'

'So you did,' I replied. 'I knew that, because I actually saw you playing for them. You see, deep down, I am a Grimsby Town fan. I used to go to Blundell Park. I remember you as a young player; Charlie Wright was in goal; Jimmy Thompson played right back; you played left back, and then the halfbacks were Ron Cockerel, Keith Jobling, Brian Clifton, and the forwards . . .'

'Don't worry about the forwards,' said Graham Taylor, interrupting me. 'That'll do for me. You know a bit about football, and I'm very interested in the possibility of involving you in chaplaincy.'

Richard and I exchanged looks, and thought this was positively hopeful, but then Graham made a comment: 'But religion is a funny subject, people get very touchy about it. I need to think about whether this is the right thing for Watford at the moment, and I'd like to see what the Board feels about it. I'll take this idea to the Board. I'll tell them about our conversation, and your willingness to be involved, and I'll see what they say. I'll give myself time to think. I'll come back to you with a decision. It won't be long. It'll be in the next two or three weeks.' I felt quite disappointed. Graham, himself, was going to talk to the Board, and after our short conversation I did wonder whether he knew enough about football club chaplaincy to make a good case.

I suggested tentatively to Graham that, if he wanted to talk to the Board about chaplaincy, it might perhaps be worthwhile my coming along to explain the precise job and role of the chaplain to them. He smiled, and said, 'Look, I think I've got the drift of what you're saying, and I'm quite happy to talk to the Board about it, but I will let you know a final decision, don't panic.' He shook us warmly by the hand, led us out of his office and down the corridor. We mounted the steps and made our way back to our church. I really felt quite down, because I had spent a good three weeks thinking and pondering about football club chaplaincy, and I wasn't sure whether Graham Taylor would put the idea across appropriately to his

Board of Directors. The whole thing was out of my hands, and I felt unhappy about that. In retrospect, that was a wonderful experience because it wasn't me trying to push or convince the Board. It was out of my hands, but it wasn't out of God's hands.

Ten days later, when Graham raised the issue at the Board meeting, I understand the Board was very supportive. There was one member who was perhaps not a committed Christian, but what we might term a 'social Christian' who went to church occasionally. Considering the situation Watford were in, he thought it would be a very good thing to have God on their side. Another Board member, who had been in the armed forces, remembered, with appreciation, the role of the chaplain in the army and felt having a padre working with the staff at Watford Football Club would help players and non-players alike in certain situations. A third member of the Board, although not a devout Christian himself, was married to a lady who was a very keen Baptist. Perhaps he felt that his wife would approve of his own personal support for the enquiry from the local Baptist ministers. Possibly for those, and for many other reasons, the Board seemed to say to Graham Taylor that, if he wanted to develop a chaplaincy at Watford Football Club, then they would be very supportive. It was only two or three days later that we received an official letter from Graham, saying that he wanted to talk to us further about the possibility. Within a few days Richard and I were on our way again to Watford Football Club to talk more to Graham Taylor about the issue.

He indicated that he wanted to see the idea working in practice before making any final decisions, but he would like us to be involved, initially, through to the end of that season.

He said: 'I do want you to be *involved* – it's not just an issue of having your name on a programme as the club chaplain. You need to be involved with this club. What I would like you to do is to come and join in training on Mondays. We meet at the Watford YMCA at 10.00 a.m. for a 10.30 a.m. start. It's an easy morning. We do music and movement work. It's a bit of a loosener, getting the lads over the aches and pains of the weekend. I'd like you to be involved in that, and I'd like you to stay around at lunchtime. We have some lunch in the YMCA cafeteria, and then we go back in the afternoon, perhaps playing five-a-side or head tennis, or something of that nature. Then you can go and visit people in the offices, see people in the various departments at Vicarage Road. You can get to know people. That's the sort of involvement I want. How does that sound?'

'Well, I used to be a teacher, and now I'm a clergyman in training, but I'm not an athlete.'

'And I'm certainly not an athlete,' Richard chipped in.

'It's OK, it's not too energetic, and maybe you, John, looking reasonably young, fit and sporty, maybe you'd stay on in the afternoon and join in when we do the more active stuff.'

'Well, I'll see, but in principle I think we'd be happy to give it a go and assess it at the end of the year.'

So, there was a general agreement that the chaplaincy would start.

The following week, on Monday afternoon, I went down to the YMCA, and was introduced to the players by the Manager. 'I'd like to introduce to you John Boyers. He's one of the ministers of the local church, and he's going to be involved as a sort of friend of the club. It's a sort of chaplaincy involvement: he's there to help and support, and be available to you, and John, along with his colleague Richard, will be coming to join us on Mondays at the YMCA. These are the lads, John, and we'll get to know you.' There was a bit of banter from some and stunned silence from others, as they met a clergyman possibly for the first time. 'I'll see you next week then,' I said and off I went.

I have many happy memories of those early days getting involved with Watford Football Club. The first Monday we turned up for popmobility made me realise the difference between my level of fitness and that of the professional footballers. I stood around with the other players in the gym as a guy came in with a dual turntable. Ken put some music on the first turntable, and, with the help of a rather athletic young lady, introduced us to popmobility. For the players, this was normal and regular. They'd got to know the music and the routines, and they energetically threw themselves into the session. Richard and I struggled with the routines, and with the fitness level. We were trying to copy what the other players were doing, and were clearly three or four beats behind everything. We realised halfway through the first record that this was actually quite hard work. When that record ended there was ten or fifteen seconds to grab a breath before a second record went on, and a second series of routines started. After three and a half or four minutes of very energetic work yet another record came on after another fifteen seconds' break. At the end of that record I staggered to the bench, gasping for breath. 'Pray for the vicar,' shouted one player. 'The Rev. needs revival,' shouted another player. 'They're on their way to heaven,' chorused a third, and there was general laughter and banter. Welcome to the world of professional football, John Boyers!

It was quite hard work fitting into that environment. The banter and chat, the joking, the 'mickey-taking' of the professional football environment was very different from anything that I had experienced either in the staff room, theological college or church, and the physical demands were also considerable. Yet, over the next two or three months, through Monday's involvement at the YMCA, and through my own efforts to start a bit of a running programme, I got fitter, and was able to do more and more with the players at Watford. Although superficially friendly the players took time to check us out, to find out what we were there for, why we were around, what our role was meant to be . . . you could see the questions written on their faces.

I think we'd been involved three or four weeks when one of the new reserve players, Keith, told us that he was going into hospital in the London Clinic to have some quite serious knee surgery. I told him that, if he would like, I could pop in to see him, and he said he would welcome that, as he thought it would be a bit lonely. So, when he was there, I went down to visit him. I took him a box of chocolates, a football magazine, a newspaper, and a little card with some Bible verses and prayers on it, and we chatted. I actually said to him: 'I will pray for you as you go under this operation. Would you like me to pray now, or shall I pray when I get back to my office?'

'I'd like to pray now,' he said, 'because I hope this operation isn't going to stop my football career before it's really got started. I do feel very apprehensive about it. Yes, can you pray for me, Rev.?'

So, there in the London Clinic, I prayed, and asked God not only to bless the surgeons but also to give Keith a sense of peace as he faced a difficult time. I returned to the London

Clinic later in the week after the operation. It seemed to have gone well, but there was to be a fortnight's recuperation in a hospital in North Watford. When I went to visit Keith there, it soon became clear that he was having a pretty miserable time. He referred to the chief ward Sister as the camp commandant, and felt the whole scenario was more like a prisoner of war camp from the Second World War than a caring hospital. 'Would you like me to see if I can take you out for an evening? You can have a meal with Anne and me, and we can watch TV together. It'll give you a break from this environment.'

'Oh! If you could do that,' he said, 'that would be absolutely wonderful, but I don't know whether the commandant would let you.'

'I'll go and see what she says,' I replied.

So, I walked over, chatted to the Sister at the nurses' station, and asked if I could take Keith out one evening to have a meal at my house, and bring him back before maybe a 9.30 p.m. deadline. She was remarkably open to the idea, and said that as long as we got him back by 9.30 p.m. there would be no problem. What day and date were we thinking of? The arrangement was made, and we took Keith home later that week. He really appreciated not only Anne's cooking but also the chance to get out of the institutional environment back into normal life again. Fortunately, Keith wasn't in there much longer. He was soon back in the charge of the physio at Watford, and made good progress from his surgery.

There was an unexpected spin-off from this situation. Keith told other players that the chaplains had bothered to visit him in hospital in London and at the recuperation hospital, and had actually got him some time out of there, provided him with a nice meal, and generally made him feel loved and cared for. The word spread that the chaplains were actually there to do good work on behalf of the staff. The role of chaplaincy began to be demonstrated to the club, and there were many other circumstances in those early days that showed we were there to help, support and befriend. Things went really, really well – and not only for the new chaplaincy.

Under Graham Taylor's leadership Watford Football Club saw increasing success on the field that season, and other significant developments off it. The provision of a family enclosure began to encourage families to come back to football. The players put in many hours of good community work, visiting hospitals and schools, meeting people at local factories, and generally raising the profile of Watford Football Club in South-west Hertfordshire. Thus, when a kit sponsorship scheme was introduced there were many local people who were willing to pay £20 to sponsor somebody's boots, or £30 to sponsor somebody's shirt, and, again, bridges were built between the club and the community.

Gradually the chaplains became an accepted part of Watford FC. We got ourselves known to the playing and coaching staff, and the office and organisational staff, and we were able to help in a variety of situations. Sometimes my involvement taught me a thing or two, too. One lunchtime at the Watford YMCA I remember joining a player who was sitting on his own at a table, munching his food. 'Do you mind if I join you,' I asked. 'We have met briefly. I'm John Boyers, the club chaplain.

'Oh yes, come and join me,' was the reply. 'Club chaplain, eh! But you're not a real vicar, are you?'

'Well, yes I am.'

'But you don't have Reverend in front of your name, do yer?'

'Oh yes I do.'

'But you're not a proper minister, not like a "Father", not like a guy who works in the church, are you?'

'Oh yes I am.'

'But you're not, what they call it, ordained . . . you're not ordained, are you?'

'Oh yes, I've got a certificate to prove that I really am a proper, ordinary, normal, ordained minister.'

'You are . . . cor. I never thought you were,' said the player. 'You seem too ordinary for that.'

I thought that was quite an interesting comment. 'What do you mean, I seem too ordinary?'

'Well, you seem too normal, you seem just like an ordinary bloke. You're like one of us, aren't you? You're not like a vicar.'

'Well, what are vicars like?' the conversation continued.

'What are vicars like? Well, I remember when I used to go to church the vicar looked about eighty-five. He wore black all over, and he was really old and bald, and doddery, and he had goofy teeth and talked with an effeminate voice. He was so out of touch I gave up going to church. It was him who turned me off totally. It was boring. He was boring.'

'Oh, I'm sorry to hear that, but you did use to go to church?'

'Oh, I used to, but I gave it up. It was boring and the vicar was boring.'

'When was that?'

'Oh, it was when I was eight or nine. I've not been since then, not really, apart from funerals or weddings.'

The conversation developed, and I went on to explain that,

for me, Christianity and Christian faith wasn't boring: it was vibrant and exciting, and it brought purpose and meaning to my life. It was a sort of foundation that I could build on, a pathway that I could walk on with certainty and security.' My comments seemed to confuse the player.

'I've just never met anyone who seemed excited about their Christian faith before. I thought Christianity was for old people or for the really young who didn't know better, but you're my age, and you're reasonably normal like me. You enjoy life and sport, yet you seem to enjoy God as well. I've never seen that in anyone, and I find that very interesting.'

I found that conversation remarkably instructive because it showed me how Christians and the Church are so often perceived. We're seen in terms of negatives: we don't enjoy this, we don't enjoy that, we don't do this, and we don't do that. So often our services, our personalities and our lifestyles seem to convince people that Christianity is dull and that faith in Christ is irrelevant. It made me realise that the Church has got a huge PR job to do, which will only be done through Christian people who live out vibrant faith through fulfilling and exciting lives. At least I was glad that the player concerned saw me as someone who was different from the boring clergy he had experienced. I had an idea that, maybe, what he saw in me and, perhaps, in other Christians, made him think again about the significance and relevance of Christian faith.

The years at Watford Football Club continued. At the end of the 1977–8 season Graham Taylor asked me if I could stay on, working with Richard, as chaplain to the club. He felt what we had done had added something to the life of the club, and he wanted it to continue. So the following season, when the club started in Division Three, Richard and I carried on our work as chaplains. The work continued to go well, and, at the end of that season, Graham asked if I might stay on as the permanent chaplain without a need for annual review. By this time I had finished my work at London Bible College, and the church had asked me if I would stay on full time as the Assistant Minister, and so things fell into place. For a day and a half each week I would have the freedom to develop chaplaincy work at Watford Football Club. At the end of our second season, Graham Taylor took the club to promotion into Division Two, and after two seasons in Division Two, we moved up to the top division. The victory chants of 'Elton John's Taylor-made army' rang out regularly around Vicarage Road.

Watford Football Club had undergone a remarkable transformation from an average mundane Fourth Division club to the top division. A young, energetic, forward-thinking manager had brought success to the club, but along with the success came criticism as some began to question the style of football that was played by Watford. Was there too much long ball? Was there too much big boot up to Jenkins and Blissett? Did Watford deserve the success they had achieved? But, footballing questions aside, for me the rise of Watford Football Club had provided a place to demonstrate football club chaplaincy, and had also provided a platform to spread the concept of this type of ministry further afield. The involvement at Watford Football Club became increasingly secure. All sorts of people felt happy about the presence of the chaplain, and through some of the good times and some of the hard times, the chaplain became very involved.

Over the years there were some heart-rending tragedies. I remember visiting one of our young staff who was taken into hospital to undergo a course of chemotherapy in order to treat cancer. Adrian was a young, fit, sporty 28-year-old, who had recently married. The news of Adrian's unexpected illness really rocked the club, and many were quite devastated when, not many months later, Adrian died. I remember that time with genuine sadness, and the chaplain was needed, not only to help Adrian's wife, but also to help the people at the club who felt his death particularly deeply.

On another occasion the birth of a baby prompted a time of huge crisis for a player and his family. The young mother had an undiagnosed heart condition and the process of giving birth proved too much for her. The baby was fit and well but the woman was rushed into intensive care, and after five or six days was transferred to Harefield Hospital where, within a week, she had undergone heart transplant surgery. Instead of the anticipated joy at the birth of his first child this top player found himself facing the daunting prospect of his young wife's life-threatening surgery. I remember visiting the family both in the Watford hospital and in Harefield Hospital on a very regular basis, and praying for them, that they would know God's grace, strength and peace. It is awesome to think that the young mother not only survived the surgery but is still fit and well today. At times like that, the help and support of the chaplain is particularly appreciated.

There were lots of minor incidents, too. I can remember a young player coming to my house, and asking my wife if he could have a word with 'the Rev.'. 'Yes, come in, Simon,' I said (Simon's not his real name). 'What's the problem?'

'It's my girlfriend, Rev.,' he said.

I immediately thought that, maybe, the girlfriend was pregnant and he wasn't sure how he would cope with it all. I offered him a cup of coffee, sat him down and asked him to tell me all about it. 'What is the problem with your girlfriend?'

'We're in love,' he said.

'Well, tell me more.'

'Well, that's it, Rev. I'm in love with my girlfriend and the club is going to release me. They're not giving me a contract, and I think I've got fixed up with another club, but I don't know whether my girlfriend will come with me. If she stays here and I go away, I just don't know how I'm going to cope. Mum and Dad are a long way off, and if I talk to the coach I don't think he'd be interested because they've released me as a player, and I can't talk to the other lads or they'd just take the mickey. I thought, I've got to talk to someone about this. Who can I talk to? So I've come to talk to you, Rev. That's all it is. I'm in love with my girlfriend, I've got to move away, I don't know whether she'll come with me. Can you help? Can you pray for us?'

We talked, and before he left I did pray. After he'd gone, my wife said, 'Were you able to help him?' I responded, 'Yes, I think so. He needed to talk, and he didn't have anyone else to talk to. It was a big issue, and who could he share it with? It was a heavy load, who else would bear the burden? I think we've just done some important work today.'

I realised that it was not only in the crises that a chaplain had a role to play, but also in the small, ordinary, almost insignificant incidents that people needed someone they could trust. I would sit in an office or on one of the seats around the stadium and have a chat, or have someone come round to the house and talk about all sorts of personal issues. They are not the sort of things that you can write about in a book because they're confidential, but I know, whether they were star players, cleaners or workers in the offices, that people at Watford really did make the most of the presence of a chaplain.

Not only was there a real sense that the chaplain was playing a part to help the club, but we were very much accepted in the life of the club. After a couple of seasons, someone realised that the chaplain and his wife had not been invited to the staff Christmas party, and they made us feel part of the club by inviting us to that. The chaplain began to get invited to a promotion celebration event at the end of each season. We were also included in the official party going to the 1984 Cup Final and to the celebration at John Reid's house in Rickmansworth afterwards. It was a little muted because Everton had won 2–0, but considering the fact that little Watford had only a season earlier finished runners-up in the First Division in their first season and had now got to the Cup Final at Wembley that, in itself, was success!

Another great occasion was Elton John's annual staff garden party, held each summer at his house in Old Windsor. All the players and employees of Watford Football Club, and their families, were invited. Elton was hugely generous to the club. He made everyone feel very welcome, posed for photographs with staff and players, and generally tried to show his personal appreciation for all that had been done to bring success to the football club. Our older son, Andrew, was very impressed by the fact that in Elton John's garden there was a big five-a-side football pitch. 'Can we have a football pitch in our garden, Dad?' he asked. There was hardly any comparison between the grounds of Elton John's mansion and our little terraced house in West Watford with a tiny concrete backyard, but we did try to set up some goals and kick into them. I am sure he very much appreciated Elton's generosity, as did everyone at Watford Football Club.

The Graham Taylor years ended in 1987. When Graham went to be manager at Aston Villa, a succession of managers came to fill his shoes. First of all Dave Bassett was brought in, but he stayed as manager for only eight or nine months. He was replaced by Steve Harrison, a previous coach at Vicarage Road, who, after a spell with Graham at Aston Villa, had returned to his old roots at Watford, to become manager. Most people would regard Steve as a really funny man who was also a great coach, but perhaps the manager's role wasn't for him. After a season and a half, Steve left and was replaced first by Steve Perryman and then Glen Roeder. Through all that period of managerial turmoil the chaplain's work continued and seemed to be valued by the players and staff at the club.

At the end of the period, a new opportunity was presented to me. It was to cause me to leave local parish church ministry in order to work full time to develop sports chaplaincy, and ultimately, it was that opportunity that took me, and the family, from Watford to Manchester.

3

Steps of Faith

The year 1990 was to herald not simply a new decade for us but the beginnings of new direction for life, work and ministry. There was no hint of this as we left the 1980s. We all felt very settled in Watford. Anne was doing some part-time teaching in a primary school quite close to where we lived and the boys seemed very happy. Life at the church was flourishing. By this time Richard Harbour, my senior minister in 1977, had left the church to lead a congregation in Didsbury. I was asked to take over his role. Life at the church was progressing well and I was enjoying working with my new assistant minister, Gareth Morris. Gareth and his wife, Liz, had been involved with the church for some years as youth group leaders and housegroup leaders when they sensed the call to theological college. The church supported them while they attended London Bible College where Gareth did very well. After college Gareth returned to us as assistant minister. Gareth and I complemented each other admirably and we felt well supported by many of the church and its leadership.

In 1989 a letter arrived from New Zealand inviting me to be one of eight or nine people who would join some suitable local clergy to make up a chaplaincy team for the Commonwealth Games in January 1990. Those liaising with the organisers of the Games in Auckland had become aware of my involvement in sports chaplaincy at Watford Football Club and knew that I had spoken at some international conferences, in Hong Kong in 1981, Nairobi in 1984, and Korea before the Olympics of 1988 on that subject. When I told, first, my family and then the leaders at the church about the opportunity, they responded very positively. A couple from the church came round to visit Anne and I to talk about the possible trip. They were very keen not only that I should go but that I should take Anne and the boys as well. As we talked the issue through, I pointed out some major hurdles. It would be a struggle for us to raise the money to get me there, as I had to fund my own flight and spending money, let alone the family. Added to that consideration was the fact that being chaplain at the Commonwealth Games was a major work responsibility: it wasn't a holiday. It would be two or three weeks' hard work extending from before the Games officially started to after their final conclusion. Perhaps, the couple suggested, Anne and the boys could join me once the Games were over? For various reasons, not least the financial one, the idea did not seem feasible.

Some weeks later the couple came to see us again with a wonderful proposal. Following recent redundancy the husband had been given quite a generous redundancy package. They wanted to use some of that money to encourage God's work and God's people. They wanted to give us a cheque to enable Anne and the boys to travel to New Zealand after the Games were finished so that we could have a holiday together. We were quite astounded by such generosity. We agreed to find out if the proposal was practical and, as it happened, the arrangements, remarkably, 'just came together.' The church was willing not only to give me time off to speak at a conference in Auckland and act as chaplain to the Commonwealth Games but also to spend a little bit of time doing some wider work that could incorporate a 'holiday of a lifetime' for the family. The Winston Churchill Memorial Trust was very interested in my chaplaincy work at the Commonwealth Games and supported me with a scholarship grant. The grant also enabled me to investigate sports ministry in New Zealand and, indeed, a little in America on my way back to the UK. Anne's school was happy to release her for a month. An old friend from theological college, Tan Boon Tong – better known to his colleagues in Singapore as Michael Tan – had always promised a warm welcome in Singapore if it was ever needed and kindly arranged a stopover both for myself and for Anne and the boys on our way to New Zealand.

The whole trip was wonderful in many ways. I remember leaving the cold chill of London Heathrow in early January and being met in Singapore by Michael Tan. He offered me warm hospitality for two or three days, showing me the sights and sounds and smells of Singapore, and we spent time reminiscing on people and situations from London Bible College days. Singapore struck me as clean, organised and vibrant. I was very impressed by the Christian work that Michael's organisation – Eagles Evangelism – was involved with, demonstrating the relevance of the Christian message to people of all cultures and social classes, and particularly to up-and-coming executives. Their use of music and visuals in large-scale presentations, and their workshops and seminars for smaller groups, seemed to be communicating the reality, the truth and the vibrancy of Christian faith in a way that was readily understood by their materialistic and prosperous multicultural society. I was also impressed by the fact that the organisation was not top heavy with those in their fifties or sixties, but was resourced by younger Christians who were nevertheless full of Christian maturity and a passion for God and his kingdom.

The Air New Zealand flight from Singapore across Australia to Christchurch and then up to Auckland was a pleasant experience. Auckland seemed slower, emptier, calmer and quieter, not only than the hustle and bustle, drive and go of Singapore, but also than the England I had left. It created an impression of England maybe thirty or forty years ago. Streets weren't filled with traffic; people weren't rushing from one appointment to another; houses weren't crammed together. New Zealand seemed an absolutely wonderful country.

Before the Commonwealth Games I attended a sports ministry conference and then met up with other ministers involved with the Commonwealth Games chaplaincy. In some respects it is quite different being a chaplain at a major games event than in a club situation. In a sports club setting you are visiting a group of people on a regular basis, maybe once a week, for a day or for a morning. Over months and years people gradually get to know you and you become part of the scenery, part of the framework of the place. They come to appreciate that you are trustworthy, they come to understand what your role and function is and how you may be able to help them. Gradually opportunities arise to be involved in ministry.

The basis for chaplaincy work at something like the Commonwealth Games is very different. In New Zealand there were broadly three groups of people who benefited from the chaplaincy. We were there to help the athletes and competitors and their entourage, we were there to be a resource to the fans and spectators and we were there to give any assistance we could to the volunteers and others whose involvement with the Games was very significant, but perhaps less obvious. At a major games event it is important that the availability of the chaplaincy team is made known and understood. We needed a chaplaincy office, we needed posters, and we needed to spend time visiting the various team headquarters. We had to make the effort to go to the places where volunteers would congregate. We had to ensure that various team leaders, whether of the various athletics teams and delegations, or leaders of teams of volunteers, knew of the chaplaincy and what it was able to offer to their team members.

Before the Games started, I visited the team headquarters from the various home countries to introduce myself. I was obviously particularly keen to support the various teams from the British Isles participating in the Games. There were teams from England, Scotland, Wales, Northern Ireland as well as from the Isle of Man, Jersey and Guernsey.

On one such visit I had a conversation with a senior administrator who seemed a little sceptical about chaplaincy work. Evidently, at a previous international athletics event, some team members had felt harassed and pressurised by well-meaning Christians who wanted to share their faith. I tried to explain my approach to him and put his mind at rest. While I believed that Christians had got something to say, I was seeking to operate as a chaplain in a non-threatening and non-confrontational way by responding to issues and situations and being available as a resource and help rather than preaching at people. That little conversation actually taught me a great deal. It taught me that zealous, well-meaning Christians can often be counter-productive in what they do and how they do it. A bad experience of Christianity, whether with an overzealous individual, or a dead and boring church, or an intolerant member of the clergy could put a person off considering the Christian message for a long time. We are ambassadors for Christ. People need to see something attractive and positive about our lives and lifestyle.

It was a great privilege to be one of the official chaplains at the 1990 Commonwealth Games, and I proudly wore the kit and tracksuit that Watford Football Club had given me to take down to New Zealand around the Athletes' Village and the Commonwealth Games' locations. On one occasion there was an amusing little incident when I attended a meeting of athletes and representatives of many of the delegations. Most people had come wearing something that identified them as part of their national delegation, with 'Malawi' or 'Lesotho' or 'Tonga', or whatever, emblazoned on the back of their tracksuit. As we chatted and socialised at the end of the meeting, an African tapped me on the shoulder, and asked. 'Where is Umbro?' I said: 'Sorry, could you say that again, please?' He said: 'Where is Umbro?' I replied, 'Umbro? I've never heard of Umbro.' He pointed to the back of my tracksuit, and said: 'It is the country you represent. Where is Umbro?' I then found myself explaining that the tracksuit was from Watford Football

Club and the kit was sponsored by Umbro, a sportswear manufacturer. He apologised greatly and said that he thought it was a small African state, and that I was one of its Commonwealth Games team. I was quite flattered really that I'd been mistaken as an African athlete. That conversation did give me a chance to explain that I was really a chaplain, and what that was all about.

Many people, including the athletes and their supporters, and the volunteers, were very grateful for the chaplaincy provision at the Games. In the evenings we took responsibility for providing a very informal prayer, praise and worship time, and I remember people like Jonathan Edwards and Kriss Akabusi coming along to join in that. Each person was very different, but each shared a very real and personal faith in Jesus Christ and, as chaplains, we were very inspired by their commitment to follow Christ in the challenging world of world class athletics.

On the Sunday after the Games finished I was given the opportunity to preach at a church just outside Auckland, sharing a platform with Kriss Akabusi. He was going to speak about how he had become a Christian, what Christian faith meant to him, and how it had changed his life. Kriss spoke wonderfully well that evening. I remember, at the end of the service, lots of young people in particular gathering round him and talking to him about being a Christian and an athlete, and about how his faith was relevant and more important to him than the medals he had won. It made me realise how important it is to have role models for young people in the Church today, They need to be inspired, not just by top sports people, or stars in the world of entertainment, but by people of all walks of life with contemporary lifestyles, who are full of integrity and have a real and relevant Christian faith.

Our time in the church that evening was quite significant for another reason too. That particular church was without a senior minister, and after the service the question had been posed as to whether I would be interested in taking the job. Anne and the family had arrived in New Zealand that Sunday afternoon. Anne attended the evening service, but listened to most of my sermon with her eyes closed, as she was suffering from jet lag. The question about the ministerial vacancy was repeated a few days later when we met with the church's leaders. Some weeks after we got back home we received a formal invitation by letter, but by that time something else was afoot.

Soon after we got back from New Zealand, another church from suburban London made contact with me, enquiring if I might be interested in their ministerial vacancy. I hadn't applied for the job, nor had I put my name forward, which is the normal procedure for finding a new placement in Baptist ministry. I knew the church. It had huge potential and was in a very pleasant part of London. I agreed to go and have a chat with the Moderator, who was responsible for overseeing the church while they were without a minister. I returned from an evening listening and talking, filled with enthusiasm. It seemed that maybe God was at work, and, the more I thought about it, the more willing I became to consider leaving St James Road Baptist Church to take on a new challenge. However, because the approach had not come through the normal channels, I decided it was important to talk to my Area Superintendent, who is a sort of Baptist Bishop looking after churches and ministers within certain regions. I made contact with Roy, and went up to Milton Keynes to chat with him.

As we spoke about this possibility, Roy's first question was: 'What would happen to all your links with sport?' I pointed out that this was a big church and the job was a huge challenge, so it would need my full attention. There would be no way that I could continue my work with Watford Football Club or my general work in sport that had grown alongside it. Roy's next question was quite challenging. 'Is that good stewardship?' he asked.

'What do you mean, Roy?'

'Well, I don't know anyone within the denomination who has had experience in sports chaplaincy as you have. You've been involved in Watford Football Club since 1977. You have recently returned from the Commonwealth Games' chaplaincy. You've spoken on the subject at various conferences and gatherings around the world as well as within Great Britain and Europe. You have done a lot of personal development and promotional work of the idea in the UK. Do you really think it is the best use of that background and experience to leave it all behind, and to focus simply on local church ministry? We have many people who would fill that local church ministry position, but I cannot think of many at all who have had your experience in sports chaplaincy.'

What are you saying Roy?' I asked.

'Well, if you're willing to leave your church in Watford,' he said, 'would you be willing to work full time to develop chaplaincy in sport? That's where I would really see you having a significant and, perhaps, unique ministry.'

'That would be interesting, Roy,' I said. 'But the trouble is, we Baptists don't have full-time sports chaplains.'

'We don't until now,' said Roy, 'but maybe now is the time we should be thinking innovatively. Maybe someone with your background should be doing this full time. Perhaps we should be looking to take you from our normal local church ministry and release you to work full time to develop sports chaplaincy and sports ministry.'

We spent some time throwing the idea around, and Roy asked if he could discuss it with the man who was then Head of Mission and Evangelism at Baptist headquarters in Didcot, Revd David Coffey. A week or so later, I had a call from David one morning. He was clearly excited by the idea, and encouraged me to look at it seriously. Over the next few months there were several meetings, some at Baptist head-quarters, some more locally in Hertfordshire and some with Revd Roy Freestone at Milton Keynes, to explore this idea and to consider ways forward.

As the idea developed I began to share it, first with my colleague at the church, Gareth Morris, then with the lay leadership, and, eventually, with the Church Meeting. It seemed to have a 'rightness' about it, and as 1990 progressed I had a growing conviction that this was God's plan. There were still many practical questions to be faced, one of which related to the issue of finance. Baptist ministers tend to be paid by the people of the church in which they serve. There is not a central pool of funds (rather a good expression for Baptists!) from which salaries are paid, but the financial gifts of the congregation usually pay for its own minister. This works admirably at local church level, but it does present difficulties when there is an opportunity to move into a para-church ministry. The Baptist Union found some money to fund the initiative for a six-month period, but there was no absolute commitment beyond that. Encouraged by my church at Watford and others, both in Christian ministry and in sport, we decided to take this step of faith and change of direction.

I guess one of the important parts of the Christian life and faith is letting God have his will and way in our lives and through our lives. That's what I had preached and taught from the pulpit for many years, and it was that which I was now faced with putting into practice again in my own life. I didn't particularly *want* to develop this itinerant ministry to the world of sport. I enjoyed being a local church minister, particularly teaching the Bible to people and explaining how to apply the Scriptures to their lives. There was a great deal of personal satisfaction in local church ministry. The offer of the job in New Zealand, in a fabulous part of the world, in a wonderfully affluent area, with many very committed Christian people, had seemed very attractive. But as I had talked the possibility through with Roy, my Area Superintendent, he had urged me to discern the difference between God's opportunity and temptation. He had said, 'I think the New Zealand possibility is temptation. It's put in front of you to drag you away from what I believe is God's job for you – this work in sport within the UK.' Comments like this were very important to me because, although the New Zealand job seemed wonderful, I think, deep down, we knew that the sporting opportunity was right.

In the spring of 1991, my local church, while still paying my full salary, allowed me to work part-time in sport, to build some foundations for a full-time work. In the summer of that year, the Baptist Union made a grant of £12,500 available to what they described as a 'strategic project' to initiate sports chaplaincy ministry. So that summer I resigned from St James

Road Baptist Church and began to pioneer the development of sports chaplaincy, initially by setting up an organisation called SCORE (Sports Chaplaincy Offering Resources and Encouragement).

Since 1978 I had been in touch with an organisation called Christians in Sport (CIS) and had served on its National Executive, acting as chairman for three years. Two of its key leaders, Andrew Wingfield Digby and Stuart Weir, had in fact been very supportive of my move into full-time sports ministry. As we worked to set up SCORE we had discussions with Christians in Sport about the possibility of this new initiative being part of their mission. Unfortunately, for mainly financial reasons, it was not possible for CIS to accommodate us under their umbrella but, through our discussions both with CIS and Baptist House, it became clear that there would be many advantages to SCORE being a registered charity.

Although at the time the decision made by Christians in Sport seemed very disappointing, looking back it was the right one. Christians in Sport have a very defined area of work and are particularly noted for their strong evangelistic ministry. Chaplaincy is not evangelism. The role of the sports chaplain and the sports evangelist are different, and I think it might have been unhelpful for me to take a chaplaincy development programme forward under the banner of an organisation known for its evangelistic work.

In those early days of SCORE, when we were trying to find a way forward, we experienced God confirming the 'rightness' of what we were doing in quite remarkable ways. In July 1991 an itinerant ministry began to develop, taking me from Watford to Yorkshire, to the north-east of England, to the north-west and sometimes far into the south-west. The miles were beginning to be 'clocked up' on our car. At that time we had a second-hand Austin Ambassador, which was pleasant enough for long journeys, but which quickly began to gain quite a high mileage. Early in November 1991 I took it into my local garage, owned by Peter, one of our church members, for yet another 6000-mile service. When I went to collect it that evening, Peter said: 'Before you collect your car, can you come into my office! We need to have a chat.' I felt a little like people must do when they get called into the doctor's surgery. Peter said: 'Sit down, let me pour you a coffee while I tell you about your car.'

'Is everything OK, Peter?' I asked.

'Well, put it this way: if it were a donkey we might be thinking of "putting it down".'

'Is it that bad?'

'Well, it can cope with little journeys around town, but these long journeys to the far north and the far south are not good for it. I think you really don't have too much left in this car with that sort of mileage. Small journeys would be no problem, but I do think you need to be looking to replace it in the next month or two.'

Peter's comments left me quite stunned. We didn't have a lot of money, certainly not enough to replace our Ambassador. 'What do you suggest then, Peter?' I said.

'Well, you might try and find a sponsored car, but certainly I wouldn't look to the Ambassador beyond the turn of the year.'

I collected the car, drove it home, and told Anne what Peter had said. I guess for the next week or two our prayer was: 'Lord, what do we do? Lord, show us the way forward.' Towards the end of November 1991 one of the leaders at St

James Road asked if I wouldn't mind clearing out my old office. The church had been very kind and had allowed me to leave all my books there – I'd not yet finished colouring some of them – but they were beginning the process of looking for a new senior minister and wanted to paint the office. One Thursday afternoon I had some space in the diary, so I took in a few empty cartons and began to pack the books away. It was the first time I'd been in the office for several months. It was quite nostalgic picking up those books, blowing the dust off and packing them away to relocate them at home.

In the midst of the packing the telephone rang. There was an answerphone there, and I was tempted to let it simply record the enquiry, but I thought, well, I am here and it does add a personal touch if there is a real live voice. So I picked the telephone up and said, 'Hello, St James Road Baptist Church office.' A voice at the other end announced: 'I want to speak with John Boyers.'

'John Boyers is no longer the minister of the church here. He resigned at the end of June, but the Church Secretary would be well able to advise you. Can I give you his name and home telephone number?' I replied.

'It's nothing to do with the church at all. I'm trying to get hold of John Boyers, I need to talk to him personally,' the voice continued.

I explained that this was John Boyers, and that I just happened to be there. The voice said, 'I really could do with talking to you. Are you free this evening? Can I see you at your home?'

'This evening I've got a meeting. I've got to be out from 6.00 p.m. to 9.00 p.m.'

'Can I see you after 9.00 p.m.?' the voice insisted.

I gave him the details of my address and said I would be pleased to meet him but before the conversation had a chance to develop any more the phone went dead. I began to wonder: I've agreed to see someone at my house at about 9.15 this evening, I don't know who it is and I don't know what it's about. What on earth is Anne going to think?

I finished packing the books, got home and checked that I was actually free that evening with my wife. 'I am in this evening, aren't I?' I asked.

'No, you've got a meeting. You said you wouldn't be back until about 9.'

'Yes, I know that, love, but I've got someone coming to see me at 9.15. I'm definitely free then, aren't I?'

'Oh, yes, I'm sure you're free later on. Who is it?' Anne asked.

'I'm not exactly sure.'

'What's it about?'

'I don't exactly know.'

She looked at me with a look that some husbands would recognise very well. 'You've got someone coming, you don't know who it is, and you don't know what it's about.'

'Er, yes, that's right, but I know they're coming at 9.15.'

'Well, I hope it works out OK,' she said.

We then got on with getting things ready for teatime.

I went to my meeting at 6.00 p.m. and returned home at 9.00 p.m. Anne was upstairs, putting the boys to bed. No sooner had I put my bags down and taken my coat off than the front doorbell rang and a young man, perhaps in his late twenties, stood at the door. He introduced himself as the voice on the other end of the phone. I took him into our front room. He sat down on the settee and I offered him a coffee that he did not particularly want. He seemed quite nervous. I asked him why he was there. 'I feel God has spoken to me,' he said. A shudder went through me. Oh no, 'God has spoken to him': is he mentally unstable? Have I brought a nutter into the house? I remember glancing at where he was sitting, and at the door, wondering whether, if he went berserk, I could get there before him. Would I be able to protect Anne and the boys upstairs if this all turned nasty? I decided to investigate further. 'You feel God has spoken to you?'

'Er, yes, that's really why I'm here.'

I then asked: 'How did God speak?' Pastorally, I thought that was a good question to ask: it would give me a real insight into what all this was about.

'I heard a voice,' the man said, quite sheepishly. 'It was sort of over here.' He held out a hand a foot or so away from his face to the left. 'It was sort of over here, near my left ear.'

Oh no, I thought. He's hearing voices. This could be difficult. The man interrupted my thoughts.

'Can I tell you something about myself? I'm a fairly logical, rational man. This has not happened before at all. It happened on Sunday evening at my church. It happened as you were preaching.' As he recounted the story, I thought, he obviously goes to church. He was obviously in the service on Sunday evening. 'What did the voice say?' I asked.

The man looked at me, and quite sheepishly said: 'The voice said, "Give your car to John Boyers." '

I must confess, on hearing this, my scepticism was reduced somewhat. I began to give the person in the room with me the benefit of the doubt. 'Can you tell me more?' I asked.

'I've never experienced anything like this before. I don't normally hear voices, and I've never ever felt that God had spoken so directly and powerfully into my life, but let me give you the background. I was given a car by my uncle, but it was a big family car, a motorway car. When I got it I was not totally convinced it was for me. I am a committed Christian, and I prayed about this car. I just had a sense that I had it for a purpose, maybe to give to someone or to help someone. At work about a month ago I was called into the MD's office, and was told that I would be getting a company car in the new year. I was delighted at this. They were going to give me a very nice suitable car, suitable for a young man to drive, but that company car offer causes more problems for me, because I'm more and more convinced that the car that I've got from my uncle is not for me. I don't need two cars. I'm not married, and I'm puzzled as to why I have this car from my uncle. For two or three weeks I have been praying seriously, "Lord, show me what I am to do with my uncle's car", and suddenly on Sunday, as you were preaching, I am arrested by this voice that says, "Give your car to John Boyers." I am sure no one else heard it, but it was clear, it was powerful and personal, and I'm convinced about it. You weren't even talking about cars . . . I can't remember how the sermon ended. I can't even remember how the service ended. I left, frightened by what I had experienced. I went home, I prayed, I opened my Bible, and it fell open at a passage that was all about obedience, about doing what God had told you to do. I was convinced that this was right.'

'Excuse me, all that happened on Sunday: it's now Thursday, why the delay?'

My guest gave two reasons. First, he was not sure how to get hold of me, and only on that morning had managed to get hold of the telephone number of the church where he knew I used to be a minister. Second, and more significantly, he said: 'I felt you would misunderstand this idea of God speaking powerfully and verbally to me: it was so foreign and so strange. It was so different. I thought you'd think I was some sort of nutter.' Then my guest asked me a question. 'Does this mean anything to you? Do you have a need for a car?' I told him about our Austin Ambassador, and how Peter had suggested it might need replacing by the new year, and how in fact, yes, I did need a car. I told him, if he wanted authentication of that, I could refer him to my man in the garage.

'Isn't that wonderful?' said my guest. 'Come on, let me take you to see the car, let me show you it.'

We opened the front door and there it was, a Ford Granada, two litre *i* Ghia, a wonderful car. He opened the door with a remote control device and invited me to sit in the plush leather driver's seat. It was better than our front room settee. The car seemed to have everything, colour television, coffee percolator – well not quite, but you got that sort of impression. It was a wonderful vehicle. The young man sat in the passenger seat. 'There's even a tape in the cassette player of some Christian worship songs for you to listen to.' It was exactly what I wanted. It was a fine, comfortable, motorway car. And he wanted us to have it as a gift. We needed to go and talk about this; we returned to the house and sat down.

I was due in Bradford the following day, and clearly it was not appropriate for me to accept the car at that particular moment. There were small matters like insurance to sort out. We agreed that he would come back on the Monday of the next week at a mutually convenient time, when we would talk over the details, but, in principle, the pair of us felt that

God was at work in all of this. He was convinced that God wanted us to have his car, and I certainly knew that we needed something to replace the Ambassador. He suggested tentatively that we do a car swap; that he would use the Ambassador until the end of the year; and that then, once he'd got his company car, he could give it away to whoever might need it. He would give us the Granada, and we would register it in our name and sort out the insurance. Within a week or two I was driving the most wonderful car that I had driven in my life.

I believe this story tells us something important about prayer and God's concern for our personal needs. I say needs rather than wants. I don't think we should treat prayer as a means of twisting God's arm so that we get what we want. When we ask for something in prayer we need to be sure that it ties in with God's will and purposes. When this is the case we can expect to see God acting wonderfully, remarkably, and sometimes miraculously.

We felt God had miraculously answered our prayers over the question of our need of a car to replace the Ambassador, but there was something else of greater importance. We felt also that God was saying, 'I am in this step of faith that you are involved in.' This whole incident said more to us than that God was able to provide us with a car: it actually said to us that God was involved in this remarkable initiative.

It was the end of November, and we knew that the money we had had from the Baptist Union lasted until the end of December. At that point in time we weren't sure what was going to happen the following year, but this whole incident gave us a confidence that God was with us, and that was very, very significant indeed. I'd like to think too that it was a great help to the young man who had given us the car as he tested out his sense of God's leading in his life, and found, through circumstances, that it was right and true. This story shows how seriously Christian people can take the call and the word of God. Christian faith is about sacrifice, commitment and generosity, and not about looking after Number One and seeking what you can gain for yourself. There could have been every reason for that man to have sold the car and used the money that he would have gained for his own personal benefit, but his Christian commitment brought everything, including his car, under the authority of the Lord Jesus Christ. What he did with it was not just his decision, but it became part of the will and purposes of God.

The provision of a car was the first of two major incidents that had a considerable influence on us as we took SCORE forward. The second also seemed to come right out of the blue. Some years earlier I'd been invited by the Secretary of Manchester United Football Club, Mr Kenneth Merrett, to go up to Manchester to talk to him and his assistant, Ken Ramsden, about the chaplaincy work at Watford. Both these men were committed Christians. Kenneth worshipped at a local Methodist church, and Ken at a local Anglican church. We had a pleasant lunch in one of the suites at Old Trafford as we talked over how the chaplaincy work at Watford had started, and how it worked. They were considering the possibility of a chaplaincy at Old Trafford, and I think they may have been sounding me out as to whether I would be willing to work on a full-time basis at Manchester United. We talked around that possibility, but I felt that Manchester United was such an influential club that it was important that they develop their own unique model of chaplaincy which other clubs could perhaps follow. Few clubs, if any, would consider appointing a paid full-time chaplain, whereas if United appointed a part-time chaplain who functioned as I did at Watford, then others could follow that pattern, using a minister with a volunteer link with the club. At that time my own church situation really mitigated against any such move, even if it was offered more formally. I was about to lose my Associate Minister, Chris Doig, to a church in Peterborough, and it would have been very difficult for the church to lose both their full-time ministerial staff within a month or two of each other. I suggested that the club might look to a suitable local minister, who could come in on a volunteer arrangement similar to mine at Vicarage Road.

I remember suggesting that a good criterion for finding the right person would be to look for someone who would be willing to be a chaplain at Bury Football Club or Stockport County Football Club. If they were willing to do that then they might have the right attitude and spirit to be a chaplain at Manchester United. I felt it was important that the individual should become involved for the job's sake rather than for any glamour linked to the football club. The two Kens used their own contacts to identify a local clergyman, and Justin Dennison became the official chaplain at Manchester United about six months after my conversation at Old Trafford. Justin's involvement was passed on to his Assistant Minister, Roger Sutton, because of his very busy diary, and Roger took on the responsibility for a two- or three-year period in the late 1980s and early 1990s.

Over the years we had maintained some contact with Ken Merrett and, when SCORE was in the process of formation, I wrote to him to ask if he would function as one of the members of a Board of Reference. We felt it was important that there were people representing both the Christian Church and the world of sport who knew of us and would be affirming of our work and ethos. Ken Merrett was ideal because he was known in the world of sport and was also a very committed Christian man. We were thrilled when Ken agreed. There he stood alongside Revd David Coffey, General Secretary of the Baptist Union; Graham Taylor, the man with whom I had worked for so long at Watford Football Club; Alan West, the former Luton Town captain who was now a minister in Luton and who had been so influential in my early days over involvement with Watford; Derek Tidball, President of the Baptist Union who was about to become the Principal at London Bible College; and John Motson, the BBC football commentator who knew of me and of my work at Watford Football Club over the years. All these men were willing to affirm their support of the newly established charity, SCORE.

We kept in particular contact with Ken Merrett, and occasionally we sent him news of SCORE along with our prayer letter, which in early 1992 sought prayer for a house move. A new minister would be coming to our old church and it was important that we moved to a new area, to get out from under his feet. So we needed to know where to live. We assumed we would move to somewhere within striking distance of Watford, and that I would remain chaplain at Watford Football Club.

It was then that Ken Merrett made contact again, and asked whether we would be willing to move to Manchester. Was this the right time for me to come and be chaplain at Manchester United Football Club? For various reasons Roger Sutton could no longer continue his role – not least the fact that the Senior Minister at the church was about to move and he would have some considerable responsibilities in the next few years. At a meeting at Old Trafford, Ken Merrett suggested that it might be appropriate for me to come north with my family and do for Manchester United what I had done for Watford Football Club for about fourteen years. I went home, promising that I would pray seriously about it and try and understand whether this was the right next step.

I must admit I was very unsure about the possibility at first. It seemed wiser to stay with Watford. I had worked with them for a long time; people had got to know me, trust me and accept me. I was part of the framework. Moving to Manchester United would mean starting from scratch. It was a big club with such a vast staff that it would be very difficult establishing a new chaplaincy work there.

However, I gave the idea some serious thought and I picked the brains of a few people. I remember talking to Graham Taylor, who, by that time, was England Manager. His advice was to check that there was a real job to do. I did that with Roger Sutton who encouraged me to say yes to the job, and felt that it was not simply a title on a page, but that there was a real opportunity to be involved week-on-week as a chaplain to the club.

I also went to talk to Bertie Mee, the former Arsenal Manager whom I'd got to know when he was Assistant Manager at Watford. In the late 1970s Graham had seen the need to have someone that knew the London area football scene, and had brought Bertie Mee in as his right-hand man. I had got to know Bertie and his wife, Doris, quite well at functions of the football club and on my regular visits round and about at the club. I remember being in his office once when the phone rang, and he picked it up and said: 'It's Mee, is that you?' I thought, what a brilliant line! In his house in Southgate, North London, Bertie encouraged me to be positive about this opportunity. 'I know you're well established at Watford,' he said, 'but really there are few better clubs to go to to develop chaplaincy in sport than Manchester United. You can model chaplaincy there in a way that you couldn't at Watford Football Club. If you and the family feel happy about it I'd really "go for it".' I found that very helpful advice.

However, perhaps the most significant advice I received was from Alan West. Alan, by this time, was Minister at Luton Christian Fellowship, and we had continued to keep in touch. Alan's perspective was slightly different to others because it was the view of a Christian minister. However, Alan was equally convinced that this move was right. 'It's a wonderful opportunity,' he said. 'God has opened a door that is a very significant opportunity for you.'

'But Alan,' I said, 'it means uprooting the family, moving to Manchester, probably increasing the mortgage. It means Anne losing her job in the school in Watford and that is a safety net for us at the moment. Are you really sure you think this is right?' Alan looked at me, and said: 'I believe God is in this but it requires a step of faith. I believe God will honour you if you take this step of faith.'

Maybe, just maybe, God was leading us to Manchester. That evening, as Anne and I talked about that conversation and the other conversations I'd had, we tried to discern God's way forward. Her comment was that we had prayed about the opportunity, we had sought God. We had actually had a look at houses in one or two other areas, but had not felt at peace in our spirits about them. We had prayed for God's guidance and this was the feedback we were getting. Other people had said it was right. Maybe it was right; maybe we should at least make some steps forward and pray that God would either confirm the move or block it. As we thought and prayed along those lines this seemed the right thing to do. I made contact again with Manchester United, explaining that if we could get our house sold and find somewhere suitable to live in the North-west, if we could find schools for the children and sort out the other necessary arrangements, then we would be happy to come.

Kenneth Merrett confirmed that they would be happy to have us, and prayed that God would open up the way forward. So we began to take concrete steps: to put the house on the market and to find suitable accommodation in the North-west. I remember talking to our young lads about this possibility. I explained to them that we felt God wanted us as a family to move to the north-west of England because God wanted me to be chaplain at Manchester United instead of Watford. My elder son, Andrew, was then about eleven. His eyes nearly popped out of his head and he said, 'Will we get to see Manchester United?'

'I think we might, Andrew.'

'You mean we'll really see them, we'll get tickets for games?'

'It might be a possibility,' I said.

'In that case,' said Andrew, 'we really must do what God wants and move to Manchester.'

I guess that was our feeling as well. We had been happy as a family in Watford, but if God wanted us in Manchester then there was no better place to be.

I continued my work with Watford Football Club until August 1992. At the final match that I attended as their chaplain, Anne, the boys and I were summoned into the Boardroom and presented with a lovely piece of crystal to acknowledge my fifteen years of chaplaincy work there.

We left Watford with a mixture of sadness and expectation. The club had been tremendously warm and welcoming over those fifteen years, and we had made some very good friends. I really appreciated the support that we had received right across the club for what we were trying to do. There was a genuine sadness that we were leaving behind the family feel that had been there for much of my time at the club. However, we knew that there was a job to be done in the North-west and there was, equally, a sense of excitement about the new challenge at, what some would say, is the greatest football club in the world – Manchester United.

4

Manchester United – The Chaplaincy

Remarkably, the move went forward very quickly. At a time when houses in Watford were falling in price, we were able to sell our three-up three-down terrace in wonderful West Watford to a couple moving out of a maisonette in Harrow. We found a suitable house in Sale in the south-west of Manchester.

Although we moved up to Manchester at the beginning of September, we weren't able to move straight into our new home. While the legal and financial formalities were being finalised, we lived with some friends from Altrincham Baptist Church, the growing and lively church we soon joined and which was, and has continued to be, very supportive of us and our work with SCORE. The Bartletts lived in a large three-storey Victorian house in Altrincham and they kindly gave up the second floor to us as a family. We lived with them for a month and we are so grateful to John and Thelma and their family for their kindness to us at this vital stage in our move.

We soon felt quite settled in south-west Manchester although the new accent and dialect did sometimes cause confusion. When finally the day came for us to move into our new home, on 1 October, I remember waiting outside the house for the former owners to complete their last bits of packing. The husband saw us in the car and came out to it, saying: 'I'm sorry to mither you, we won't be long.'

'Sorry, what did you say?'

'I'm sorry to mither you, but we won't be long,' he repeated.

I understood from the sense that 'mither' must mean 'hassle', 'to be a bother', 'to be a pain or a difficulty to', and yet it was a totally new word for me, but one that is, quite clearly, regularly used up here in the north-west of England. Learning new words and dialects was nothing new particularly. Anne is originally from Sunderland and, in my early visits to that part of the world, I would have found a lay person's guide to 'mackemese' very helpful. Equally, I am sure, she struggled with some words that were basic to my Lincolnshire upbringing. I can remember Mother saying to me as a child: 'Come on, let's tidy up this kelter,' or my father commenting on the rain outside, saying, 'It's absolutely siling down out there.' Words and local expressions have always fascinated me, and we soon came to understand some of the North-west's idiosyncrasies. They also had to get used to ours. I remember asking Jonathan, who was then seven, how he had got on on his first day or two at school. He seemed to indicate that he was fine and people were friendly, but he was surprised at one boy asking him if he was Australian. Evidently, Jonathan's strong Watford accent had been misunderstood by one of his classmates. 'Tell him your father's come up here to develop a kangaroo farm, Jonathan,' I said with a twinkle in my eye. Evidently, Jonathan had already told him that I had come up to be chaplain at Manchester United. That was a line that both he and Andrew were happy to use when their school-mates enquired about their dad's job. In the past it had not been very cool to have to admit, 'My dad's a church minister'. I remember once discussing this with the lads when they were young, and saying 'You can always say, "My father works for, or is a friend of, the most powerful being in the Universe" but they didn't seem to feel that was too cool either. However, being able to say their dad was chaplain at Manchester United, particularly in very red South Manchester, did, I was told, give the boys some 'street cred.'

Anne spent the first three months or so trying to get the boys settled into their new home and into their new schools, and generally getting our new home organised. We decided that that was our priority, rather than seeking another teaching job for her, although we knew that would be important in the medium term. Our move to the North-west was actually quite a challenge to our faith. Although SCORE was develop-ing well, our financial foundation was not particularly strong. In those first eighteen months we always seemed to have enough money in the kitty to keep going for another two or three months but we never had an abundance of funds. We could never feel peaceful and contented about our financial situation as an organisation, but we had been happy to live with that because Anne had a full-time teaching job in Watford which had eventually become a permanent contract. I had said, more than once, to our SCORE treasurer that if there was not enough money in the kitty to pay me my full salary, the organisation should pay me what it could, as we had Anne's salary to fall back on. However, the move to the North-west was a real challenge for us because it meant that we were deliberately saying goodbye to the safety net of Anne's salary. It was a big step of faith, but we believed it was the right thing to do. We believed that all the details, including our finances, would fall together. Again, in that we saw the goodness of God. Several weeks after we had arrived in the North-west, we saw an advert in a free newspaper. A local primary school needed a part-time teacher. As we read the details in the paper, it seemed just the right job for Anne. She applied for it, and despite being an older teacher, who was a little more costly to the school than someone straight out of college, they offered her the job on a one-year contract. Her link with the same school has continued and grown, and for that we are very thankful. So, the family settled in, and I also settled in to working from a base in South Manchester. I began to make that regular and rather slow four-mile journey up the A56 from Sale to 'The Theatre of Dreams' as part of the developing chaplaincy work.

Before moving up to the north-west of England and actually getting involved with Manchester United as their chaplain, it had been important for me to clarify certain matters with the club. First, in discussion with the Secretary, Kenneth Merrett, who was very sympathetic with my views, I made it clear that my chaplaincy involvement was for the whole club. In my view the chaplaincy should neither focus exclusively on the playing side of the club, nor equally on the non-playing side. Both were important. The chaplain needed to establish a rapport with those on the playing, coaching, management side who related to team matters as well as with those on the administrative and organisational side who related to non-playing matters.

It was also important for me to know that the Manager was equally supportive of my proposed style of involvement. Up until then I had not met him, nor spoken with him, and had not had the opportunity to outline my ethos of chaplaincy to him. It was agreed that I should meet him one Wednesday when we were up in the Manchester area checking on schools and houses. I had been told that he was an incredibly busy individual, particularly on that Wednesday, because United were at home to Chelsea, and it would be unlikely that I would have much time with him. I was also warned that his strong Glaswegian accent made him quite difficult to under-stand.

My initial meeting with the Manager was, however, a very warm and positive exchange of views. Alex Ferguson was clearly supportive of the chaplaincy concept and saw the need for the chaplain to work confidentially with all of the staff at the club. He understood that all types of staff would, from time to time, be confronted with situations that might broadly be described as pastoral or spiritual, and that some of those would find the availability of a chaplain helpful and supportive. I explained that I didn't expect to help all of the people all of the time, nor did I expect to have an automatic involvement with those struggling with personal, home, health or domestic difficulties. I think I used the phrase 'pastoral and spiritual safety net' to describe the role and function of the club chaplain as I saw it.

I described my involvement at Watford Football Club and explained that I would envisage the chaplaincy at Manchester United working in much the same way. I wanted to get to know the staff and help them understand who I was and what my task was and to be available to them as much or as little as they wished. For some people my presence would perhaps be an irrelevance, while for others it would be an important resource.

I also wanted to explain to the Manager that he wasn't opening a door for some wild preacher to come into the club and confront his staff with his own Christian beliefs. I hoped he would trust me not to bash his staff over the head with a Bible. However, if people at the club began to ask me spiritual questions, I felt I must have every right to respond by express-ing my opinion and understanding. I explained that I saw my spiritual input as broadly reactive rather than proactive. I stressed I didn't want to impose my beliefs, my faith onto people who didn't want to know. I wanted the staff to feel safe when the chaplain was around. However, I wanted to empha-sise that the chaplain was more than a social worker. There were times in people's lives when they needed some input at a spiritual level, and, if that was appropriate and sought, then I needed the freedom to give it. Again, I found the Manager helpful, open and affirming. 'That's what the chaplain's for,' he seemed to be saying. 'You're not there as a "Bible Basher", but if people want to talk to you about spiritual things, about God and faith, then I'm very happy for you to listen and to respond appropriately.'

That meeting was quite important because I felt I had support from both sides of the club, from the administrative side and the playing side. As a consequence of that meeting I really felt happy about our move to Manchester United.

The club had offered me tickets to watch the League game against Chelsea and so that evening we returned to Old

Trafford. I took our older son, Andrew, who must then have been eleven years old. Roger Sutton, who was then the chaptain, parked in one of the car parks, and took us across to what was at that time the Family Stand. It was in the corner between the South and East Stand. We went through the turnstiles, mounted a long series of steps, and came in at the top of the stadium. It was then much smaller than it is now, seating 44,000 people, but it was much bigger than anything we had been used to at Watford. As we entered the stadium, we were confronted with an awesome view of a huge round bowl that looked absolutely magnificent under floodlights. Andrew's eyes opened wide. He was obviously thrilled and amazed at the magnificence of Old Trafford. The game was not bad: it was a 1–1 draw against Chelsea. I came away thrilled at the opportunity to attend the match, but realising too that this was a very big club indeed. I wondered what it would be like to actually work here as chaplain.

On one occasion I shared with Anne my concerns about getting established at such a big club with such a large staff. I very much appreciated her wise words. She said: 'You mustn't see this in the same light as Watford. You must remember what it was like at Watford in 1977. You didn't know anybody, you didn't know how the club was run; you felt very much on the outside of things, and it took you some time to get to know the club and for the club to begin to trust and accept you. It will be the same at Manchester United. Remember what it was like in the early days at Watford, and do what you did then, up here in the North-west.' That was remarkably good advice.

I did simply try and get myself known at the club as the new chaplain. Ken Merrett's secretary took me round several of the offices at Old Trafford and introduced me to some of the departmental heads. The Manager introduced me to some of the players and staff at the Cliff training ground. I recognised that for the most part the next six months would be hard work as I tried to get myself known.

My pattern of work today has not changed a lot from those early months of the autumn of 1992. The club has probably doubled in size. There are now about 550 full-time staff associated with Manchester United Football Club and on a match day perhaps another 1500 come in to work part time. The stadium is much bigger, and new extensions to the East and West Stands will take the capacity to a total of 67,500. There are awesome restaurant facilities: one banqueting suite in the North Stand can seat 1000 people and another in the West Stand can seat 750. On a match day perhaps 5000 five-course meals are prepared, and about 14,000 pies or pasties sold. The Museum and Tour Centre is a focal point for fans all over the world.

In 1999, following the club's unique Treble achievement, 273,889 people came to look at Manchester United's Trophy Room and to tour the stadium on one of the official tours. Each day in the summer holidays forty-two tours, lasting an hour and a half, take fans from all over the world around the club to look at features of the stadium, including the Police Control Room, the Manager's 'dug out' area, the changing rooms, the players' lounge, the famous 'Tunnel', and much more besides. Even out of school holiday time, the club seems a hive of activity, not only with tours to the Museum and Visitor Centre, but also with commercial and business gatherings in many of the suites which enable Manchester United to offer superb conferencing facilities for businesses and commercial organisations. In addition, the merchandising side of the club brings in a regular flow of visitors to the Megastore where so much Manchester United produce can be purchased. It is a huge and successful business institution, as well as being a football club.

As chaplain I could conceivably work at the club seven days a week and still wonder how to have time to fit everything in that could be done. As it is, I give the club about a day and a half each week. Monday is my normal day for visiting the club. I try to start around 9.45 a.m. when I visit departments and offices throughout the club. By about 11.15–11.30 a.m. I'm back in the car again driving to the training ground where I usually pop into the physio's room – to see the sick and dying! – chat to people there, and then talk to others as staff come back from training. A bite to eat around the dining tables at the training ground is followed by a chat with staff and players.

Then I head back to Old Trafford where, usually around 1.00 p.m., I meet with Ken Merrett and Ken Ramsden. Together with a few other committed Christian members of staff, we talk about the issues, not necessarily to do with football, that are current for that week. This Christian fellowship meeting usually takes place in Ken Ramsden's office, whether he is able to be there or not. It is not a meeting that prays for success for Manchester United, but is simply an opportunity for the staff to pray together for needy situations – some connected to the club, others not. For some of the Christian staff at the club it is an oasis where they can think more spiritually than perhaps they have the time to do within their normal responsibilities. Our conversation might range from issues relating to the Third World to what we found particularly helpful within our churches that weekend; from moral or ethical issues relating to sport, or perhaps to society generally, to what has happened at Old Trafford over the days since we last met together. It is a helpful forum to discuss issues relating both to the world generally, and particularly to the football world, from a Christian perspective. We always try and bring our discussions to a conclusion by about 1.45 p.m. so that we can spend a few minutes in quiet meditation and prayer. We bring to God our praise, our thanks and our intercessions for those we feel are in need.

Then it is out, back into the normal life of Old Trafford again. I continue my rounds visiting people in many different offices, calling on people like Lyn, the Manager's PA, and her assistant, Hilary. I talk with Keith Kent, the groundsman, and his staff, then visit those who are in the Group Property Services department, the maintenance staff, and those involved with the commercial side of the club such as staff at the Megastore. There are a host of other people who each make a contribution to the commercial and organisational life of Manchester United within their particular departments, like Adam and Simon, who manage the website and Cliff who edits the match programme. Round about 4.00 to 4.30 p.m. the day's work is drawing to an end, and I begin to head for home.

My work on a Monday is essentially contact time with the staff and people at the football club. There are often a couple of significant conversations during the day, but most people who want to talk about a personal issue prefer to do so in privacy. Therefore, sometimes I'm asked if it's possible to meet to follow up a conversation at some depth, and either we meet at someone's home or in a quiet corner of the club. I've often used an executive box, for instance, to chat with an individual who wants to talk privately outside of the confines of his or her office at Old Trafford. At the training ground area, I might sit in a car with one of the staff to talk through whatever is on the individual's mind.

I am also aware that it is an information-gathering exercise. As I walk around the club, I might hear about someone whose mother is critically ill or whose daughter is going into hospital, or who personally might have to face surgery. This is information I am then able to act on.

There are a number of situations in which I think a chaplain can be particularly helpful, such as times of illness or hospitalisation when he or she can visit both at the hospital and at home. At times of bereavement, too, many people appreciate the support of a chaplain, to offer pastoral support to those grieving, or even to conduct a funeral.

Of course, there are happier occasions too. Sometimes people seek advice about weddings, and a few years ago I conducted a wedding for a couple, Alan and Barbara, who worked at Manchester United. The evening before the ceremony we had agreed to meet to have a rehearsal, and I'd suggested to my wife that I might be home by 9.00 p.m. just in time to pick our younger son up from his youth group. Some of those involved were delayed, and, as a consequence, our rehearsal did not get started at 7.15 p.m. as we had anticipated. At 8.15 p.m. I phoned my wife to say that I would try to get back for 9.00 p.m., but if she could sort out a lift for our son perhaps she would phone me – I would leave my mobile on. The rehearsal continued. I was going through the Order of Service and came to the point where I asked if there was anyone here present who knew any reason why these two persons may not lawfully marry. Just as I had finished that question, and as a quietness and a hush descended in the building, my mobile phone rang, to the great consternation of everyone present. When I answered it I found it was Anne. The wedding party had a huge giggle about that. 'Has God got a reason?' one of them asked, with a wry grin on his face. The next day at the wedding proper, when I came to those significant words, the Best Man caused his mobile phone to ring with a smile at me, much to the guffaws of all the party. Of course, I had to explain what was going on, but it really broke the ice, and I think Alan and Barbara enjoyed their wedding, as indeed did many of their guests from the football club who were there. Days like that are very special.

But that sort of thing is the occasional rather than the normal. The week-on-week work of the chaplain is to get alongside the ordinary people of the club and to listen and to respond to needs and situations as appropriate. You are there to help people, but you are far more than a social worker. Often people need not just help, support and counsel, but help at a spiritual dimension. When faced with the loss of a parent or a child people may value an arm round the shoulder, but I find they need more than an analysis of the grieving process. I believe people have found it really helpful to have the chaplain pray, share some words of Scripture, and talk about Christian hope. When I visit people in hospital I often ask if I can pray with them there, or if they would feel more comfortable, I could pray for them when I get back to my office. Most people are quite happy for me to pray with them in hospital, particularly if it is before the operation! I have been interested in how all levels of staff from the club seem universally to be open to, and appreciative of, this spiritual level of support and input.

Perhaps this indicates something of the nature of our humanity. I often speak about humankind as having five aspects to our being. We clearly are physical people: we have a body in which we live, and the health or otherwise of that body affects all of us, but we are more than that. We have a mind, an intellect, and a capacity to think, but we are more than body and mind. We are also emotional people: we love, we hate, we are happy, we are sad, we are angry, we are pleased. So, there is body, mind and emotion. But there is also a social dimension to our life: we are social creatures, we like to be accepted, and we like to be in the company of others. We find purpose and meaning in relationships. Some people we like, others we dislike. I believe, too, that we are spiritual creatures. We have a spiritual dimension to our lives: that is how God made us. That is what distinguishes humanity from the rest of the animal kingdom. Humankind has a spiritual dimension that causes us to be aware of the greatness and goodness of God, to be aware of a spiritual realm in a way that the animal kingdom is not aware. They do not gather for worship, they do not gather to pray, they do not ponder what happens hereafter. However, humanity is different. Universally, in all societies, there is evidence of that spiritual dimension, that seeking after the One who is God Almighty, the One who is Higher and Greater and Stronger than ourselves. We are spiritual creatures.

The truth is that our spiritual dimension can be ignored, it can be filled with the wrong stuff, or it can be filled with that which God intended. I believe God wants us to experience the life, light and power of the presence of his Spirit within our lives. Christianity is not just like a club. The Church was not intended to be just an organisation. At the heart of the Christian message is an explanation of how, through Jesus Christ, humankind can find forgiveness and wholeness that brings the very life of God's Spirit into our lives here on earth. Christianity seeks to show us how we can find the Spirit of God coming into our lives to make us new people, God's people. So, the Christian faith is not only about believing truth in our heads, but it's about experiencing something of the truth, the power and the life of God within our spirits. God invades our spiritual dimension.

It is this understanding of the five aspects of human nature, including a spiritual dimension, that is one of the main reasons for the significance of chaplaincy work. Much of that work is friendship, caring and supporting, but there are times when genuine friendship, confidential care and consistent support are not enough. There are times when people need spiritual help and spiritual input. At those times the chaplain is both a pastoral and spiritual safety net. When a lady finds that her husband is diagnosed as being terminally ill with three months to live, she may find spiritual input more important than anything. When a young married couple find that their longed-for and expected baby has died, they need spiritual help too. When a woman who, in the past, has had an abortion cannot find any peace or escape from the guilt that she feels inside her, then help at a spiritual level might be required more than anything else. When a family are confronted with bereavement, and yet have no particular church link and want someone they know to take their funeral, then the chaplain's availability becomes particularly significant.

Equally, life may throw up situations and circumstances

when the chaplain's perspective may be sought after, such as the death of Princess Diana. That tragic event led to a number of people at the club challenging me over how God could allow pain and suffering in the world. I was interested to see what sort of people were asking the question, and how widespread it was. Some people say that we live in a society that has grown out of the need for church or belief in God or Christian faith particularly, and yet I believe that certain events in life trigger the deep questions that perhaps all of us have.

I suppose there are seven or eight common questions that I find people confronting me with on a reasonably regular basis. One would be about the existence of God: why do you believe in God? How can we know that God exists? Another question might be about personal significance: why are we here? Where do we go to? Are we just beings for a moment of time, and then we disappear, or is there some eternal aspect to our being? If there is, how do we find our real purpose for living? The third question is one that we have already mentioned in this book: the question of suffering. People will often ask: if you believe in a God who is all-powerful and all-loving, why does suffering happen? Why does God allow bad things to happen to nice people? Why is there pain and tragedy in this world? A fourth area of questioning would be about the significance of Christianity as opposed to other faiths and religions: does it matter what you believe as long as you believe something? Do all religions lead to God? Are all beliefs equally valid? Arising out of that might come another particular question for those who hold Christian belief: the question about the Church or the Bible. Why should we take Christian faith seriously when those who belong to the Church seem to undermine Christian faith and lifestyle with their lives, their statements, and with the way they live? There is another question that is often pointed to Christians as well. It is about the basis of faith: why should we believe the Bible, why should we give it any special significance? Isn't it just a collection of old fables, stories from ancient history? Why should we consider that it has any relevance for society in the twenty-first century? Then there is the question that arises out of the text of the Bible itself: the question of miracles and the supernatural. If we live in a rational and mechanistic universe, how can we believe in a God who is supernatural, and who works in miraculous ways? How can we believe that, in the life, work and ministry of Jesus Christ, God could apparently suspend laws of nature? How can we believe, in a rational world, in a faith that is based in the death and resurrection of someone who Christians claim is the Son of God? These are the regular questions that are thrown up by the ordinary people who live and work in and around our sports clubs, and who, from time to time, think about the spiritual dimension in life.

Now is not the time to answer all, or any, of these questions. There are some excellent books which deal with these issues, but I do believe that the Church needs to be listening to the questions people are asking, and making a reasonable and cogent Christian response. If the first lesson I have learned from my chaplaincy involvement at United is that there is a real and spiritual dimension in life, then the second lesson is that we need to be listening to the questions that people are asking. I think, generally, the Church is very good at providing answers to questions that people aren't asking. If John and Sally have suffered the tragic loss of their little baby, their question may be: 'How can there be a God if this sort of thing happens?' The Church needs to be empathising with them where they are at. Yet, so often the church says, 'Believe in Jesus, confess your sin and you will be forgiven. He will give you new life and you can know God's love personally.' Those statements may be true, but they may have no bearing at all on the questions that John and Sally are actually asking about the loss of their beloved baby. The Church today must learn to scratch where people are itching.

Perhaps that brings me to my third lesson from chaplaincy, which is that we need to be where people are. I don't have a special 'chaplain's room' at Manchester United where people come in to see me. I am not averse to the idea of having an office that I might be able to work 'out of', but I would never want the chaplain to be sitting in a room where people come in as and when they need to. It is far more significant and, I believe, theologically far more valid for me to go where people are. The Christian faith is the story of the God who has broken out of his glory and come to meet the needs of a broken and damaged world. In theological language the 'Jesus event' is called the 'incarnation'. God came amongst humanity in Jesus Christ. In his life and in his ministry Jesus went to where people were, and Jesus called his disciples to follow in his footsteps and to do the same. We are to go into the world. We are to be 'salt and light' in our society. One of the great lessons that I've learned from football chaplaincy relates to the need for the Church to move outside of its walls and windows, and to be involved in the world.

Sport is not the only world that we need to be involved in. We need to be involved in the world of education, politics, business, commerce, finance, culture, arts, drama and music. Church services are important. They are important for worship and Christian fellowship, for teaching and encouragement, and as places where the injured and the hurt can find grace, strength and restoration. I am not minimising the significance of God's people meeting together. However, we must not allow our meeting together to become our only function as we seek to serve God. We need to serve God in the world, and into that world we bring not only a Christian perspective, not only a Christian outlook, but also integrity, truthfulness, honesty, goodness, compassion, kindness – Christian qualities that the world needs. We need to balance its greed with our sacrifice, its taking with our giving. I believe Christians who have got a passion for Christ and his kingdom, who are concerned for mission, need to espouse again the fact that social action and social involvement are equally important for those who seek to follow Jesus Christ and serve him. We need to remember again that some of the great saints of the Christian Church in years gone by were those who were very committed to social involvement. The Earl of Shaftesbury was involved in prison reform as an expression of Christian faith; William Wilberforce was involved in the abolition of the slave trade; William Booth was involved in helping the poor in society. Our Christian faith must be seen to have a social outworking. It is clear from Ephesians 2 that we are saved to do good works, to be socially and pastorally involved in all aspects of our society – not least, the world of sport. It is a privilege we must not shy away from.

Another great lesson that I have learned from football chaplaincy is that the Church needs to be involved in the world in a way that the world can appreciate and understand. During my time as chaplain of Manchester United there have been occasions where the special functions of a Christian minister have been seen to be particularly relevant. I think, first, of the time when Sir Matt Busby died. I had met Sir Matt on two or three occasions as he sat in his old office at Manchester United Football Club, puffing his pipe and reading the newspaper. I had come to realise the huge affection and the great respect that was given to the man who had rebuilt the club in the post-war period. His death was announced on a Thursday, and that evening I was due to play with some of the staff from the merchandising department in the all-weather gym at the Cliff training ground. When we arrived and talked together there was clearly a great sense of sadness at the news, and we even wondered about the rightness of going ahead with our game. I suggested to one or two that it might be appropriate for us to start with a minute's silence and perhaps I could say a few words. As we gathered around the centre circle, with our opponents, I introduced the minute's silence, and after it offered an impromptu prayer. It was clear to me that many of our team, just ordinary members of staff broadly taken from the merchandising division of the club, were deeply shaken and upset by the sad news.

Over the next few days I spoke with many members of staff about Sir Matt, and people were eager to tell me of their happy memories. I enquired at the club whether it would be appropriate for me as the chaplain to be at the funeral, but was advised that it might be more helpful if, on the day of the funeral, I could stay behind to offer support to the staff who would be left back at Old Trafford. This I did, and many people talked to me on that occasion. Those of us who were there will never forget the crowds and the sombre silence as the funeral cortege made its way from the church to Old Trafford, and then on to the burial. The tributes that were left to Sir

Matt, the scarves, flowers, mementos, and the deeply respectful and affectionate comments made by those who had worked with him and under him, will never be forgotten.

At the memorial event at Old Trafford, organised by the club, I was asked to say some prayers as the club chaplain, and I was pleased to do that. It was a privilege to be involved and to hear wonderful testimony to Sir Matt's goodness and kindness, as well as his firmness and managerial abilities, from the Busby Babes and others who knew him.

Another major service in which I was involved was the Munich Memorial Service held in Manchester Cathedral in 1998 to commemorate the fortieth anniversary of the day that is so poignant and tragic in the history of Manchester United and indeed in the story of British football. Ken Merrett, Ken Ramsden and I met up with the Dean of Manchester Cathedral to consider what particular elements to include in the memorial service. We eventually agreed on a broad outline, and again I found myself actively involved as the club chaplain in leading some prayers. I spent time composing special prayers for that occasion, and was glad to have had the opportunity to serve the club as one of those involved in the service. Both of those events were sombre occasions, but another major service was in contrast full of joy and exuberance.

In September 1994 *Songs of Praise* came to Old Trafford. One of the *Songs of Praise* producers, John Forrest, had made contact with Manchester United, via Kenneth Merrett, to talk about the possibility, and I was brought in on it a little later. The BBC wanted to use the football ground to hold the biggest *Songs of Praise* congregation ever. The idea was to use a corner quadrant of the stadium, with a band on one side and a choir on the other, to accommodate four or five thousand people. As Kenneth Merrett, Ken Ramsden and I discussed the proposal, we felt excited at the possibility of being involved in the biggest *Songs of Praise* ever, and allowing the facilities of Manchester United to be used for this 'one-off' occasion.

At the press conference held in one of Old Trafford's conferencing suites some months before the filming of the event, one of the clergy present asked if seats could be reserved, and, if so, how many could be claimed. There was slight amusement as it was pointed out that we were looking to have four or five thousand people from the general public present and the ground held 44,000. However, it turned out to be a very relevant question because the BBC soon became inundated with requests for tickets for *Songs of Praise* at Old Trafford. At one stage 2000 tickets per day were being sent out to churches of all denominations right across the United Kingdom. Soon the 44,000 seats were all allocated and a waiting list of 15,000 had been set up for people who would be willing to take tickets should any returns become available. I understand that another 10,000 requests were simply told there was no chance of tickets being available. The idea of *Songs of Praise* at Old Trafford had captured the imagination of the Christian public across the UK. As their chaplain, even I got several telephone calls, one from down in Essex, enquiring if I could get any tickets for the programme. I pointed out that I was the chaplain and not the ticket office, but they thought that I might have some influence. I followed my normal practice when anyone asks me for tickets for anything, and referred them to the normal ticketing mechanisms.

It was a terrific day, but a real worry for some of the

members of staff at Old Trafford because the event was much bigger than anyone ever imagined it would be. When the band struck up that afternoon there must have been 30,000 people within the stadium, and another 10,000 still waiting to take their seats. It was an interesting event from many points of view. When I spoke to the men on the turnstiles in the week after, one of them said how strange it had been to see people coming through wearing scarves from different football clubs, but not shouting, swearing, fighting or being aggressive. 'It was very odd,' he said, 'but the atmosphere was very different. It was wholesome; there was a sense of happiness and goodness and kindness about the place. It really was quite remarkable.' I've often thought about that, because I do think that Christians should make an impact wherever they are, in the ways they live and behave. Here was an ordinary man working the turnstiles who felt the overall impact of this gathering of Christian people contrasted distinctly with the sort of atmosphere that a normal cross-section of the public provided as they went through the turnstiles at Old Trafford.

Some of the contributions made by sports people during the recording of the event itself were also very powerful. Both Phil Starbuck and Vai'iaga Tuigamala, who then played for Wigan Rugby League Club, spoke about their faith and their involvement in sport. (Phil's story is included in more detail in Chapter 8).

Phil had started his football career at Nottingham Forest, making his debut for them at the age of eighteen under the management of Brian Clough. His early years in football were particularly successful, but he left Forest to go first to Huddersfield Town and then to Sheffield United, and ended his professional playing career at some of the lower League clubs. Phil stood up and explained how, in what turned out to be a fairly average and unspectacular career, his Christian faith was important and significant. His commitment to God had remained strong and real despite the ups and downs, or in his case, downs and downs of the life of a professional footballer.

Songs of Praise at Old Trafford was a great event. I was asked to say a short prayer of benediction that was recorded as the final prayer of the TV programme. When that had been done I was allowed to pray more freely in my own words. I prayed a prayer thanking God for the occasion, seeking his blessing as many people left to travel home, and praying that the broadcast would be effectively used to speak of the reality of Jesus Christ and in some way extend the kingdom of God.

Formal services like the ones I have mentioned are quite exceptional events for a chaplain. All of them were the result of a unique situation or a special set of circumstances, but they did provide an opportunity for me, as the club chaplain, to be involved in a more formally religious setting, and for that I was thankful.

More recently a new area of involvement has opened up for me in the life of the club. In 1997 SCORE was contacted by the Footballer's Further Education and Vocational Training Society, known as FFE and VTS, which is the educational wing of the Professional Footballers' Association and is run under the auspices of Micky Burns. They were in the process of preparing a new educational scheme for younger professional footballers, which was to be called the Adidas Football Scholarship Scheme, and would replace the two-year Youth Training Scheme. The idea was simply to provide a three-year educational scheme that would prepare young footballers much more broadly for life.

Micky explained that about 50 per cent of the players who enter football at sixteen were out of the game by nineteen and another 50 per cent of those who were there at nineteen had left the game by the age of twenty-one. This huge drop-out rate, accounting for 75 per cent of the young players between sixteen and twenty-one, was a cause for great concern. They felt a responsibility not simply to provide training for a career for the 25 per cent who remained at the age of twenty-one but also to provide a foundation for life for the 75 per cent who would be out of the game by that age.

They knew that there were many young people in football whose focus for their lives had just been on becoming a YTS trainee at a football club and then a professional footballer. Yet, for many of these aspiring professionals, the future may not have been all that they would have hoped. Some would be told that the game probably would have no place for them, and there would be others who probably had the skill, personality, determination and character to make it in the game but who, because of injury, would have to find another source of employment. There would be another group of players who would make a living in professional football for some years and then at maybe twenty-eight, thirty-two or thirty-five would need to find another full-time job. The average career span in professional football is only seven or eight years. It is a very short career, and many of those who leave professional football do so without huge financial resources behind them. For people such as these, the Professional Football Association (PFA) saw a need to provide a broader foundation for life, and they were seeking to bring this in through the Adidas Football Scholarship Scheme, and particularly some key educational units that would take place within that scheme. Micky wanted to find out whether we thought chaplains might have a role to play in this scheme, and, in particular, if we could input into two areas: pastoral care and personal relationships.

I had thought much about the role of chaplains in providing a wider education for young players particularly. My involvement with Watford Football Club had led me on a much more informal basis to try to provide something that might broadly be called educational for the young players at the club. Over the course of a year I would take them to a West End theatre in London to see a play; I would take them into London to see some of the historical sights; we would visit a local restaurant and speak about the cutlery and how it is used for different courses, and how you deal with ordering food in a higher quality restaurant than some of them were used to; I would take them out socially, often to a ten-pin bowling rink in Harrow where we tried to develop social skills and talk about interpersonal behaviour. We also had groups of the Watford apprentices round to our home periodically for a bite to eat and a bit of a chat, and we might look at something like a *Fawlty Towers* video. Throughout all these activities we were trying to build some foundations for living and provide some perspectives on life that went beyond the young players' experiences in football. I was, therefore, delighted when FFE and VTS made contact to talk about the Adidas Football Scholarship Scheme, which seemed to be seeking to address that very same problem.

They asked SCORE if we could create a syllabus for the two subjects of 'Pastoral Care' and 'Personal Relationships', and provide some resources for chaplains to teach the syllabus to the young players within the clubs. I was particularly heartened that the PFA's attitude was not simply to try to 'get the information over to the young people'. They saw the real benefit in the scheme as building a bridge between the chaplains and the young footballers, so that as those players were confronted with difficulties, problems and challenges later on, they could find support through the chaplain. I have worked personally, on behalf of SCORE, to produce not only the outline syllabuses for the unit on 'Pastoral Care' and 'Personal Relationships' but also outline lesson plans for the chaplains, to enable them to communicate the approved material without too much bother or problem. We use video and overhead projection slides to provide a reasonably fast moving, varied and interactive lesson for the younger players.

As a teacher I had had experience of courses in PSHE (Personal, Social and Health Education) designed to give students in Year 11, 12 and 13 the information that would help them in their future lives, by studying topics that were relevant to real-life situations. This is what we are trying to do for young footballers. We tackle topics like friendships, sex, prejudice, bereavement, social maturity, pastoral care, bullying, coping with success, coping with failure, how to make good decisions, the issue of responsibility – topics which will be helpful whether the youngsters are able to stay in football or not. Our material is designed to help them enjoy learning information, skills and attitudes which will provide foundations to their lives as adult members of society. As a Christian minister, I find it enormously encouraging that a professional body like the PFA came to SCORE to seek its help and advice, acknowledging Church might have something to contribute in this particular area of life.

As part of my chaplaincy work at Manchester United I see

the outworking of this locally. Our Adidas Football Scholarship Scheme members are involved with Ashton-on-Mersey
School in Sale. The school has an excellent reputation locally,
and is one of the Government-designated sports colleges. The
headmaster, Mr Tarun Kipur, is very supportive of the involvement of the Manchester United scholars, who attend the
school all Monday morning and all day Thursday. United's
Education and Welfare Officer, Mr Dave Bushell, helps co-
ordinate the educational side of the Adidas Football Scholarship Scheme, taking responsibility for the organisation of the
lessons. Two or three times per term, in my capacity as club
chaplain, I visit each year group to give some input. This is
just one of the ways that United tries to look after its up-and-
coming players.

I have been really impressed by the way the Manager and
his coaching staff seek to identify and nurture young talent
and train them for a life of professional football. However, I'm
also very aware of the Manager's personal concern for the
wider welfare of his young players. He sees them not simply
as players on a football field but as young people for whom
he feels a real responsibility. His interest in their progress at
the local school and his support for myself as the club chaplain
are just two examples of his concern for the wider education
and development of the youngsters under his charge. He seems
to want these young lads to succeed in life as well as in football,
and he is keen for them to develop good habits that will help
them as they grow into maturity. He sets great store on
standards, on appropriate attitudes and on right behaviour.

At the training ground recently I was sitting in the dining
room having a bite to eat, talking with some of the coaching
staff, when the following incident happened. The Manager

came in and saw one of our young Adidas Football Scholarship players tucking into his lunch wearing his training sweat top, which was obviously still damp from his work in the gym. He was injured and had worked hard in the gym for a couple of hours rather than being involved with the rest of his squad at the training ground. Sir Alex asked the question: 'Have you been working in the gym, and have you had a shower before coming in here to eat?' The player looked at him and said: 'Yes, I've been in the gym, but no, I haven't got showered.' It was obvious to all that he hadn't. The Gaffer looked at him again. 'You know the rules: you shower first before you come and eat, now go shower.' The young player left his food, got up, went down, showered, changed and then came back to finish his meal. That little incident spoke to me of the Manager's concern for standards and for people. He wants the best for those involved with Manchester United Football Club.

In all my dealings with people at Manchester United Football Club I believe confidentiality is of absolute importance. The club chaplain must be known as someone who can be trusted. If a member of staff shares a personal detail with me, then that has to be treated with absolute confidence. People need to know that information they share with me is not going to find its way back to the club Secretary or the club Manager.

Sometimes I may feel, however, that the information I receive needs to be conveyed to someone else in a position of authority within the club. In such cases I would talk to my clients first of all. I would emphasise that I would not break their confidence, but that, because of a certain set of circumstances, I felt it was important that they shared that same information with the person who was, in effect, their head of department. I can think of a situation involving one of our younger players, some years ago, with whom I spoke one evening about personal circumstances that were troubling him considerably. I asked if he had spoken to the Manager about the problem. The young player explained that he wasn't sure how the Manager would react, and felt that it was perhaps better not to say anything to him about it. I tried to explain that I thought it was important for the Manager to know about the situation, and, if the boy wanted, I would be willing to be a go-between and organise a meeting. However, I promised him that I would not say anything unless I had his permission. The young player said that he would be happy for me to represent him to the Manager, and that he would be willing to talk to him if I would attend the meeting with him. He asked me to make contact with the Manager. To cut a long story short, I got in touch with the Manager one Saturday night and met with him about 8.00 a.m. the next day in his office at the Cliff training ground. We talked over the situation and arranged for me to bring the young player in to see him the next day to talk it through. Over the next week or two the Manager played an active part in getting the situation resolved. For me that was a very satisfactory outcome because, although I felt that the Manager needed to know of the situation, it was important for me to maintain my integrity.

This stress on confidentiality explains why in a book about chaplaincy and work with Manchester United Football Club and Watford I can only talk about the generalities of the chaplain's day. At both clubs I've been given the privilege of working with, and alongside, some very high profile personalities and many wonderfully 'ordinary' people who are not household names. To the international superstar and to the ordinary staff member I, like every other chaplain, must be committed to confidentiality. There can be no exposure stories. The chaplain has to practise what he preaches. As a minister your lifestyle has to be congruent with your beliefs and your teaching. There is no point saying one thing and doing another. Integrity is vital. I do hope the world can see in those who are Christians a lifestyle and an integrity that is compatible with their faith. The chaplain has to live out his faith too. If he speaks of confidentiality, then confidentiality must be an integral element of the way that he works. If he speaks of consistency, he must be consistent. If he speaks of compassion, he must be compassionate. If he says the part-time cleaner is as significant as the international player is, then he must show that in his attitudes and in his commitments. I want chaplains to be seen as reliable and valued servants of all who are involved with their clubs.

We need to 'debunk' some of the myths. We are not witch doctors praying for success. We are not 'sports mad clergy' who are living out some faded dream in the guise of chaplaincy. We are not 'hangers-on' who are trying to get free tickets for games, autographs for our families or famous visitors to our church fêtes. It is important that the chaplain is always seen as someone who gives more to the club than he takes from it.

5

United – A Religion?

My first season, 1992–3, was a good one to join United. The previous season they had been in a very good position to win the title, but had been pipped at the post in May 1992 by the Cantona-inspired Leeds United. The 1992–3 season healed the pain and anguish of the previous year. I enjoyed watching United play some great attacking football, but I was particularly impressed with their positive forceful climax to the season. I'll never forget the game on Easter Saturday, when United played Sheffield Wednesday at home; Steve Bruce had equalised an earlier Wednesday strike and headed a courageous winner in the sixth minute of injury time. This sent Alex Ferguson and Brian Kidd leaping onto the pitch with delight, and 40,000 United fans into ecstatic rapture. It was an amazing finish to a game that had seemed lost, but was won with determination, character and no meanness of skill. I think that result led many at Old Trafford to believe that 1992–3 really would be our year. One of the *Match of the Day* commentators remarked in that game that United had come back from the dead. It was quite an appropriate comment at Easter time. They won away 1–0 at Coventry on Easter Monday and momentum gathered as the season came towards its final few games. A 3–0 win at home to Chelsea consolidated their position and it all rested on that crucial Saturday when, while United were winning 2–0 away against Crystal Palace at Selhurst Park, Aston Villa lost 3–0 to Blackburn at Ewood Park. United's main rivals for the championship were beaten. United were the champions for the first time since 1967. The atmosphere amongst the staff at the club was electric. People were so thrilled that the hard work and dedication of Alex Ferguson, his coaching staff and the players had, at last, gained fair and just reward. The final match of the season, was to take place on the following Wednesday evening against Blackburn Rovers. Instead of it being a championship decider, it was to be the game at which the new FA Carling Premier League Trophy was presented.

On the Monday before that final game of the season I was doing my normal rounds at Old Trafford when I met Ken Ramsden, the Assistant Secretary, who invited our whole family to come and be part of the celebrations. 'Would you like tickets for yourself and Anne and the two boys?' he enquired.

'That's very kind of you, Ken. We'd be delighted to come as a family. I suppose we'll need to be there about 7.30 for the 8.00 p.m. kick-off, won't we?' was my response.

Ken looked at me a little strangely and said: 'I think it'll be a very, very big occasion. There will be huge crowds here. Do please try to get here early. I recommend you try and get into the staff car park for 6.00 p.m. I think it'll be a bit special on Wednesday night.'

We had an early tea that evening, decked ourselves up in the red, black and white of Manchester United, and made our way down to Old Trafford, quickly at first, but as we neared Stretford and then Gorse Hill the traffic slowed. By the time we got to the staff car parking area we were down to crawling pace. I was amazed at the scene on the forecourt.

It seemed as though there were 50,000 people outside the ground. There were flags and balloons and banners – proclaiming loyalty both from local supporters, and from those from much further afield in England and as far away as Cyprus, Malta and beyond. The sense of euphoria was amazing. There was shouting, singing, chanting and dancing. I had never seen anything like it before, certainly not at Vicarage Road, Watford, nor Blundell Park, Cleethorpes.

We edged our way through this excited euphoric mass of bodies into the car park where we got out and took a moment to 'drink in' the atmosphere. I remember Anne saying: 'It's sad really, isn't it?' I looked at her, incredulous. 'It's what?'

'Sad,' she said. 'It's sad, isn't it?'

'No, it isn't, love. It's happy, they are really, really happy.' And I turned to the boys, 'Hey, lads, tell Mum these fans are happy. There's nothing sad about this.'

'I was just thinking,' she said, 'it's sad because all this excitement and euphoria is all about a football match.'

'All about a football match!' I said. 'This isn't just any football match. This is United. This is United winning the League. This is United winning the League for the first time since 1967. This is twenty-five years of hoping and waiting, twenty-five years of frustration and disappointment being overcome with success. All this is happiness.'

As we walked towards the crowd, and through them towards the turnstiles, I remember thinking that Anne never really did understand football. As we mixed and mingled through that bubbling jubilation of ecstatic fans, I did come to see what Anne was saying. For some of these people it was as though the Holy Grail had been found, as though cancer had been cured, as though the problems of Third World poverty had been solved, or as though war had been overcome by peace . . . The atmosphere was incredibly euphoric, but I thought, Anne is right. It's a wonderful achievement, it's a great evening, but it is only a football match.

For many in that crowd there was something almost religious about their fervour, and that made me think deeply about the links between following a football team and what we would call 'religion'. Indeed, some sociologists have even suggested that football is the 'new religion'. There are certainly some interesting parallels. Our magnificent stadia have been described as the 'cathedrals of our day'. Many of them are brilliant architectural structures, and they are without doubt the focus of regular pilgrimage for thousands. It is interesting to reflect that the two places where, more than anywhere else, adults gather to sing together are our cathedrals and churches and the sports stadia of our nation. There is singing and there is worship in both, and it is with some consideration that I use that word with reference to our sports grounds. It really does seem to me that some fans do worship their heroes, and give them a status they hardly deserve. At many grounds we have seen fans mimicking the idea of bowing down in devotion and obedience, in a sort of expression of submission and worship. Most of us understand that it's only done for a laugh, but it is, none the less, indicative of a very real attitude amongst some sports fans. They really do endow their favourites sports stars with almost godlike characteristics.

There are other religious parallels as well. Where once people used to dress up to go to church, we now find people dressing up to go to a football event. They may dress up informally in the club colours with scarves, jumper, tie, and the rest of it, or even very formally, if they are using their executive boxes for business purposes, or if they are using their involvement with club hospitality facilities for more commercial reasons.

For some, weekly attendance at a football match provides an ingredient in their lives which others find in the church. In church we speak of Christian fellowship, in Greek *koinonia*, describing the spiritual and social camaraderie that assures you that you're one of a group who care for you and support you. Something of that can also be found in the seats or on the terraces of the football ground. At a football match you meet the same people; you get to know them; you ask how Simon's brother is, and if he got over his operation in hospital. You see Jack and Margaret, and enquire how Margaret's mum is getting on. By virtue of being in the same place at the same time on regular occasions, there is an interest and a depth of relationship. In a society that is losing a sense of community, people are finding something meaningful within their area of the stands or seats at the football grounds.

There are further parallels between the sporting world and religion. Consider the sacrifice of those who are followers. The Christian gospel challenges us to take up our cross daily and follow Christ. This means being prepared to give up everything that might prevent us from giving our utmost for him. My understanding of the Christian faith is that we become actively involved in a huge exchange: on the one hand the fallen nature of my character, my wrongdoing, what the Bible calls 'sin', is dealt with through the death of Jesus Christ on a cross. I experience the benefits of the punishment which he suffered for humankind. As Charles Wesley wrote in one of his hymns, 'His blood avails for me'. But, on the other hand, there is another exchange which has to be worked out daily: the exchange of my will for God's will. Just as Jesus said that he came not to do his own will but to do the will of the One who sent him, we, as Christians, now belong to the kingdom of Christ. Now that we follow Jesus who is the Lord, we have to allow that lordship to have a daily impact on our lives. So my preferences – what I think, how I want to live, how I feel – become subservient to the will of God. Christians live, not as they would individually choose to live, but in the way that they believe God would want them to live. To be a Christian is to live a life of sacrifice – we give up our will for God's will.

This to me, a Baptist minister, is expressed supremely in the service of Baptism. The New Testament message speaks about acknowledging one's sinfulness, and repenting, that is, turning away from living a selfish life and consciously seeking to turn to God's way. We believe that, through Jesus Christ, forgiveness can come, and that there can be new strength as God's Spirit breaks into our lives to help us live God's way. Baptism is a sign that the old life has ended and that God has begun a new life within us. Baptists don't believe in adult baptism; they advocate believers' baptism. The act of immersing a believer under the water and then lifting them out is not symbolic of a 'washing', but is symbolic of a 'death' and a 'resurrection'. The old life has gone and a new life has come. It is symbolic of what God has done in that individual, and what we believe God will continue to do within that individual. Believer's baptism by immersion is a symbol of personal Christian sacrifice. I am no longer my own, but I belong to Christ. My old life with my desire to live it has died, because I am now a new person in Christ, and I am seeking his way for my life from that moment on.

Football fans sacrifice a great deal to support their team. Their commitment is amazing. Whether it is Plymouth Argyle fans supporting their team in Hartlepool, or Carlisle fans following their team down to Brighton, they are prepared to travel great distances simply to watch the game. Your see it on every match day on the motorways. A cynic will tell you that a large proportion of Manchester United fans travel up from south-east England to watch their team. Revd David Coffey, the General Secretary of the Baptist Union of Great Britain, once told me this joke: 'How many Manchester United fans does it take to change a light bulb?' The answer, of course, is two: one to change the light bulb and one to drive him up from Essex. There is also a Baptist angle on that joke. How many Baptist deacons does it take to change a light bulb? The answer to that is: 'Change? Baptist deacons don't change anything.'

The commitment of the fans is costly. It costs money to buy the tickets, let alone the programme, food and drink before or after a game, overnight accommodation at some away matches, and transport. Sports fans who are committed followers of their team make sacrifices in terms of time and finance. Sacrifice and commitment are important and central Christian concepts, but yet, around our sports stadia, we see people who sacrifice as much or more than those who sit in our Christian congregations. We see people whose commitment to support their team sometimes outshines the commitment of Christian congregations to attend services of worship or midweek housegroup meetings or church prayer meetings and the like.

The world of sport also challenges the Church with its passion. Look around the stadium before a big game, and there is a sense of excitement, there is atmosphere, there is anticipation. You can see passion on the faces of the supporters. Sometimes I am saddened by the lack of passion shown by Christian people. I think there should be times when being in the presence of God in a service, perhaps particularly at a major Christian gathering, really does touch our emotions as well as our spirits. Sometimes that can happen quite quietly: we feel the powerful gentleness of God around us; we become aware of his awesome holiness; we feel humbled, we are quiet, we reflect with wonder in our hearts. There may be other times when we feel a vibrancy and an excitement; we have a sense of God's power and God's majesty; and we begin to anticipate that God is at work. As Christians we need to communicate our excitement about God's reality. Jesus spoke about the purpose of his coming: 'I am come that you might have life, and have it in all of its fullness.' Do Christians reflect that fullness of life to the world? Is there a sense that we have found the answer? Is there a sense of purpose and power? Is there a sense of reality and vitality? Is there a sense of genuine truth and integrity about our lives?

What is more, do our church services inspire those who occasionally come in? I heard a lovely story about a lady who decided her son was old enough to be taken to church. He was quite a lively little chap, and as they walked towards the entrance of the church she said: 'Now you must be quiet, now really be quiet.' As they went through the church door she emphasised to him: 'Be quiet, shhh.' As they made their way along the pew he started to talk, but his mum said: 'Be quiet, shhh, shhh.' When they got into the pew she knelt down, and he started to ask why she was kneeling, and again she said: 'Shush, be quiet, kneel down.' In the end the bemused child couldn't cope with this any more, and said: 'Mummy, who are we hiding from? Maybe we should run away now?' Perhaps, at some of our services, that is the impression we give.

Church can be perceived as boring, and sadly irrelevant to normal life and lifestyle. The greatest joy and happiness in the service can come when we actually escape from it. I remember a lady at the door of my old church in Watford once saying to me: 'John, thank you for your sermon today. I enjoyed it, I particularly enjoyed the end of it.' When she'd gone I thought, that could be taken two ways, couldn't it?

We really do need to convey something about the relevance, the reality and the excitement of Christian faith as well as the parallel truth of its challenge and significance for humankind. It is an interesting reflection on our society that words like 'fellowship', 'worship', 'commitment', 'passion' and 'sacrifice' are as much at home in the context of a football team or a sports stadium as they are in a church building amongst a congregation of Christian believers. It confronts the Church with the truth that we now live in a post–Christian society. Over the past forty years society has changed enormously, and people today just do not have the close contact with the Church that they did a generation or so earlier. This is not necessarily a major problem for the Church. Those who confess faith in Christ now are not doing so for social or cultural reasons. People who live a lifestyle that demonstrates that they put Jesus Christ first today do so simply because they really believe it. There are no social norms to follow.

Since we are no longer living in a society where people flock to church, we must take the message of the truth of Christ from the Church into the culture in which we live. Mission is about 'being sent' out of the Church into the world, and I believe chaplaincy involves individuals in mission in the very fullest sense of that word. We go as representatives of Jesus Christ and his Church to the world, and we go to that world as servants. We are there to help, to be available, to show compassion, to be true and genuine people; not to impose, not to threaten, not to corner, but to serve. The Scriptures tells us that we should emulate the servant attitude of Jesus. Jesus was the suffering servant who fulfilled the prophecies in the book of Isaiah. He was the humble servant who took on the menial task of washing his disciples' feet in order that they might learn from his example. He was the obedient servant who chose deliberately not to do his own will, but to do his Father's will. We remember his supremely significant prayer in the garden, 'Not my will, but yours be done'. Jesus also is the saving servant. Through his service comes salvation to all who hear his voice and respond to the call of his gospel. Here, again, is something for the Church to grasp: the significance of service in society, service in community. By adopting his attitude of compassion and servanthood we can reflect something of the life, the truth and the reality of Jesus to the world in which we live. We know that not everyone will see it, and not everyone will respond to it, but so it was with Jesus Christ himself. Many saw his servanthood and mocked him for it, not least in his greatest act of service for humanity, when he hung on a cross at Calvary. The crowd shouted: 'He saved others, now let him save himself'. The truth was that in that very place, by remaining there on the cross, by choosing not to save himself, he made it possible for others to be saved. His service became a channel for the salvation of others.

I really believe that there is a principle here for the Christian Church today. If we serve our society with integrity, in godliness, in the way that God, our Father, desires, we will be able to release the reality of his salvation into the lives of many people. Paul's letter to the Ephesians tells us that we are saved to do good works. Christians should show their faith to the world in acts of service and of love. What chaplains do in football clubs can be paralleled by ordinary Christian people in their own communities and neighbourhoods. When talking to churches I sometimes differentiate between chaplaincy practice and chaplaincy principles. When I speak about chaplaincy *practice*, I talk about the chaplain's day-to-day involvement in a football club, rugby club, or cricket club, for example. I might also speak about the more unusual opportunities he might encounter. Then I try to demonstrate how the chaplaincy *principles* can relate to ordinary Christian people as they seek to serve God in their own personal ways.

Let's take an example of Derwent Drive, an imaginary cul-de-sac of maybe twenty-five or thirty houses. Let's assume that there is a Christian family living in that cul-de-sac who have a concern to reach out with the love and truth of Christ to other people. They might ask: how can we communicate our Christian faith to our neighbours in a way that is acceptable – that doesn't threaten? Now let's use our imaginations to wander around Derwent Drive.

At number 3 there is an old lady, a widow, who has been on her own for some time now, but is finding increasing problems with the garden. At her age it's quite difficult for her to get the lawn cut and keep on top of the weeding and pruning. Here is an opportunity for the Christian family to say: 'Can we help you? Is there anything we could do practically? Could we run our hover mower over your lawn once a week? Could we in the spring and autumn prune some of the trees and bushes? If you need it dug over occasionally, we'd be happy to do that for you.' In this way they can express their care and concern for that individual.

Let's move across the road to number 12. The family who lives there are going through some major difficulties. The wife has already spoken to our Christian mum about some serious marriage problems, and even spoken about a possible divorce. That might be a signal that the Christian family needs to provide some help and support. If the couple need some time on their own they could take the children off their hands for a day or for a weekend. They could invite the husband and wife across for a meal. They might try to get together with the husband and wife and begin to talk about counselling facilities available through organisations like Relate. Instead of watching the family disintegrate through increasing and unresolved tension, the Christian family can be actively involved in giving support and help.

Let's move a little further down Derwent Drive to number 18. A happily married couple, in their early fifties, lives there. Suddenly, right out of the blue, the husband has a heart attack, is rushed into hospital, and dies. The wife is left devastated, grieving over her lost husband who seems so cruelly to have been taken away from her. She is very uncertain about how she will cope because both her children now live away from home and are busy with their own families. This situation again presents the Christian family with an opportunity to try to get alongside the newly widowed neighbour to offer help, friendship, support, companionship and, again, possibly some support and counselling through specialist agencies such as Cruse or other similar organisations concerned with help and support for the bereaved.

At number 23 is a family with three children. Mum and Dad are in their early forties. There is a real concern for the younger daughter's health. She has recently had two spells in hospital. She is suffering from problems in her brain function which seem to be affecting her movement and her general development. The hospital is monitoring the situation and more tests are in progress, but Mother and Father, quite understandably, are very worried indeed. Let's assume that the Christian family, because of a local school link, knows this family. They've met and talked as they've come back from school together with their children and are very aware of the illness that is threatening the child. Again, this is an opportunity for the Christian family to show their concern, perhaps by sending a bunch of flowers or a card offering some prayers and readings, or promising to pray for the situation. Perhaps they could offer to help with transport, or in any other way that would be useful.

This is a fictional scenario, of course, but it probably isn't far away from reality. In all our streets there are families who are facing the strain of childhood illness, marriage breakdown, parents or partners who are terminally ill, or situations where unemployment, financial strain, health matters or bereavement have cast a huge shadow over family life. Christians can offer care, support, friendship and help at vital times. I believe that this style of involvement is both culturally relevant and socially acceptable to people in our present post-Christian society.

Chaplaincy practice might, by and large, be for ordained clergy working in particular secular situations. However, chaplaincy principles can be followed effectively by many Christians working in their own particular communities and neighbourhoods. They can get to know people, they can show their genuineness and their concern. They can eventually become trusted people, who can offer help and support. They can bring in a spiritual dimension when it's appropriate, but not be heavy or pushy or threatening. They can pray for those that are in need, and then they can sit back and wait to see God at work in the situations they have been praying for.

Let's go back to our big football stadium on a match day, whether it is Anfield, Old Trafford, Elland Road, Stamford Bridge or Highbury, or indeed, Blundell Park. There are certain parallels to religious life, and we have discussed that earlier, but it is important, equally, to see the other side. Christian faith confronts humanity with answers to some of the biggest questions of life. 'How can I ever forgive myself?' 'Why am I here?' 'Where do I go to?' 'How can I cope with the strains and stresses that I am under?' The atmosphere and life of a football stadium may take our minds and thoughts away from these big questions of life, but when the game is over we find those questions still remain. Sport may be like a religion, but it doesn't get to the heart of our problem.

I believe Christian faith does get to the heart of our problem. It confronts our basic needs effectively, eternally and hopefully. We all know that we fall short of our own standards, let alone God's. We all know that we do, think and say things that are wrong, and Christianity offers to all of us a way of forgiveness. The question, 'how can I forgive myself?', is answered in the fullest way: you can forgive yourself because God, in Christ, offers you forgiveness. More than that, God, through the Holy Spirit, comes to live within you, to strengthen you and help you when you become a Christian. God's love and forgiveness becomes something not simply for the mind, but something that touches our hearts. Wesley's great hymn 'Love Divine All Loves Excelling', speaks in the language of earlier generations of the divine love of God breaking into the human heart: 'Love divine all loves excelling, joy of heaven to earth come down, fix in us thy humble dwelling, all thy faithful mercies crown.' God transforms us through his love, grace and power. We become adopted into his family, redeemed and set free from all that would bind and hinder us and prevent us from experiencing the fullness of his truth and love.

We become new creatures. The old does indeed pass away, because something new has come. God has illuminated our darkness with his divine and eternal light. There is no parallel to this sort of thing in football. The trappings of Christianity, the outworking of religion, aspects of the life of faith, worship, fellowship, sacrifice, commitment, passion – all these might be found in sport, but there is nothing that the fan can experience that is like Christian conversion. Far, far better than watching your team win away is the knowledge that you are loved by God, and that his love and truth in Christ has taken you out of darkness and brought your spirit and soul into light that will surround you forever.

6

Training, Teamwork and Transfers

From a very young age I was introduced to the parables of Jesus, and I came to appreciate they were special stories. I still remember the definition of a parable that I was taught at Sunday school. It is an earthly story with a heavenly meaning. The parables of Jesus, recorded in the Gospels, show how our Lord used the simple ideas of life to get over the complex ideas of God's truth and God's kingdom. Take, for example, the story about a sower. Everyone was familiar with the idea of a sower sowing his seed on land that had been prepared for cultivation. They knew that some areas of the land would be rocky and others would be invaded by thistles and weeds; they knew there would be a pathway where the soil was too hard for the seed and where the birds would snatch it away. Jesus's image of the sower was so familiar to them. They understood it, and yet it contained a strong spiritual challenge. If the seed is like the word of God, what sort of soil are you?

There were parables about sons who argued about their

inheritance, and about a man on a journey who was waylaid by thieves, and helped, of all people, by a Samaritan. There was a simple little story about a mustard seed that is so small but when it begins to grow and take root, it produces a plant that is so big that even birds can roost in it. Two of my favourite stories which seem to explain the nature of the kingdom of God better than anything else are Jesus' stories about the treasure in the field and the pearl of great price. A man ploughing a field stumbles across treasure that has obviously been buried there for a long time. He does not own the field, but is so desperate to own the treasure that he sells everything he has so that he can buy the field and therefore be the rightful owner of the treasure. In the same way, a pearl merchant comes across a unique, exquisite and most valuable pearl. He, too, gives up what he has in order to gain what cannot be exceeded. Jesus uses these stories to explain the nature of the kingdom. He challenges us with the truth that, if we give up what we have, we can inherit something of even greater value.

The parables of Jesus are wonderful, and we would do well to read them more regularly. Yet, I am aware that they were set in a very agricultural society which is not as relevant to our life today as it was to Jesus's listeners. If Jesus was walking around in Britain today, what parables would he tell? What images would he use to communicate the truth of the kingdom of God? I'd like to suggest to you three parables for the twenty-first century. They are about training, teamwork and transfer.

Training

Since my late twenties when Graham Taylor invited me to join in Watford's training, first at the YMCA, then a little later on at the Shendish Training Ground near Hemel Hempstead, and then later still at the North London Polytechnic Ground at Stanmore where Watford train, I've been impressed by the amount of training that goes in to make a top athlete. Every footballer obviously needs basic physical training. But in addition he needs training in skills and techniques which will help him to function both within the pattern of a team and to exercise his precise role within that team.

We know there is much more to us than simply a physical body. There are many more areas besides football skills and techniques that we need to be trained in. How, for instance, do we best train ourselves spiritually? If human beings have a spiritual dimension to their being, how do we train that dimension?

I have often used a verse from 2 Timothy 3:16, which tells us: 'All scripture is inspired by God and is useful for teaching the truth, rebuking error, correcting faults and training in right living.' A soccer coach may wish to teach the truth, rebuke error, correct faults and train his players in the correct techniques and skills of the game. Timothy says that the Scriptures do exactly that for us. If we want to be trained spiritually, then we need to study the Scriptures. The Bible is our training manual. If we are looking for a spiritual personal trainer then we must find the time to allow God to speak to us through his Word.

We all lead full and busy lives. We don't easily find time to have a walk, or to do a jog, or to go down to the gym, squash court or tennis club in order to take some physical exercise. As a family we don't have a dog, but one of the great assets of having a dog for a pet is that there are certain times of the day when you have to take it out for a walk. We actually have a goldfish; Jonathan seems to be largely responsible for feeding it. I take my share of the responsibility. I check that it swims daily – it seems to do that quite well – but that doesn't take much exertion. Even though we know exercise is good for us, it can so easily get squeezed out of our lives. Our lives are so busy that even good things get crowded out. The same can so easily happen to our spiritual fitness too. We all know it is best if we spend time, on a daily basis, reading a portion of Scripture, thinking about it, sensing what God would say to us through it, and seeking to apply it to our lives. Then, perhaps, we should be praying a little, offering prayers of worship, prayers of confession, prayers of thanksgiving and prayers of intercession for those in need. Yet, how many of us, even Christian leaders, fail to do what we know is necessary? If we wish to train ourselves spiritually we need to follow accurately our spiritual training manual.

Teamwork

A second football parable that I want to consider is the idea of teamwork. I remember once at a conference presenting to the young delegates, on an OHP slide, the names of a squad of international players chosen from the English FA Carling Premier League. It looked a formidable squad, but then I showed them two possible team formations. The first team had the players playing in their normal club and international positions. It was, indeed, the sort of team that could have won any competition in the world. The second slide showed that same squad of players playing in the wrong positions. The quality goalkeeper was playing in the centre of midfield, the strong, powerful centre half was playing on the left wing, the striker was playing at full back, and the full back was in goal. It was an absolutely stupid team, and the young lads at the conference told me so. One of them pointed out that they couldn't have expected any more football sense from a self-confessed Grimsby Town fan.

I proved my point. Within a football team there are players of different abilities and different strengths who have to find their right place within the team. That, indeed, is the essence of teamwork. A team is not made up of identically gifted and skilled people, but of people with different skills and abilities who complement each other. One player may be very strong, a robust tackler, the sort of defender who would, in football parlance, 'go through a brick wall' for the cause of his team. Another may be a player with great touch, skill, vision and a remarkable passing ability. He may not be a strong tackler or a firm defender but his creative, constructive play makes him a huge asset in a midfield position. The striker, the full back, the goalkeeper and the winger all have different skills and attributes, but when their specialisms are brought together successfully they become a team. The essence of the team is that together it is stronger than the sum of its parts. As long as the players play in the positions that are most suited to their skills and abilities, it will be an excellent team.

This picture of a multi-talented squad of differing yet complementary talents speaks to us about the nature of the Church. In Romans 12:4 Paul draws a parallel between the Church and the human body. He says:

Just as each one of us has one body with many members, and these members do not all have the same function, so in Christ, we who are many form one body, and each member belongs to all the others. We have different gifts, according to the grace given to us. If a man's gift is prophesying, let him use it in proportion to his faith. If it is serving, let him serve; if it is teaching, let him teach; if it is encouraging, let him encourage; if it is contributing to the needs of others, let him give generously; if it is leadership, let him govern diligently; if it is showing mercy, let him do it cheerfully. (vv. 4–8)

He stresses two important concepts about the nature of the Church. Unity does not mean uniformity and diversity does not mean disunity. The Church is like a human body made up of different parts or members, each with its specialist functions, each co-operating with the other parts to enable the body, as a whole, to function.

In 1 Corinthians 12:14–20 Paul emphasises that differences within the body should not be disdained, but should be seen as especially significant. He writes:

If the foot should say, 'Because I am not a hand, I do not belong to the body,' it would not for that reason cease to be part of a body. And if the ear should say, 'Because I am not an eye, I do not belong to the body,' it would not, for that reason, cease to be part of the body. (vv. 15–16)

Perhaps if Paul were writing today, or if Jesus was trying to explain something of the nature of the Church today, they would use the football team as their analogy. The football team is composed of many different players, but their differences don't disqualify them from being part of the team. Indeed, it is their unique differences that make them of value to the team.

There are at least a couple of important lessons to be learnt from this concept. The first is clear and obvious. If we are to be effective members of the Church we need to know what our real strengths, abilities and gifts are. It must be horrendous having to play in midfield if you are a talented goalkeeper. Round pegs function best in round holes. It is so easy within the life of the Church for round pegs to function in square holes, or goalkeepers to end up in midfield. It is vital for both the congregation and clergy to understand one another, so that each can function in a way which best suits their particular gifts and skills.

The second lesson may seem obvious but is nevertheless fundamental. There is room for all of us within God's team. The fact that you may not play organ or keyboards doesn't mean there isn't a place for you in the team. The fact that you may not be an administrator or organiser doesn't mean that you are excluded. Another person may struggle with 'up front' presentation, but that does not exclude them. The cleaner must be given a cleaning function; the organiser must be used organisationally; the one who is gifted in singing needs to be used in that very area of ministry. People need to hear that there is a place, a role, for them within God's team. We are not all worship leaders, we are not all Bible teachers, we are not all administrators, and we are not all organisers. We have different gifts and abilities, and we need to find out what our specific talents are. We need to know that God has room for people of varied talents in his team, and that our particular gifts do not exclude us. Equally, when we get involved in the team we need to appreciate that not all of the other team members will function as we do. They may have different strengths and complementary gifting. The truth that enables us to find our place in God's team should free us to allow others to find their own place in that same team. Diversity should not be a threat, but a strength. Teamwork amongst God's people is a very necessary and biblical concept.

Transfers

The third of our hat trick of footballing parables is the idea of transfer. Despite the huge implications of the Bosman Ruling any football fan understands and appreciates the significance of the transfer system in football. When a player is under contract to a particular club, the club owns the rights to hold his registration documents for the duration of his contract. When a transfer takes place, the ownership of the player's registration documents moves from one club to another.

I remember as a younger Grimsby Town fan feeling betrayed and horrified by the transfer of our strike force of Matt Tees and Rod Green from Grimsby to Charlton for £23,000. It was headline news one evening in the *Grimsby Evening Telegraph*, and many ardent Mariners' fans were pretty upset that two of the team's star players had been sold, but transfers take place in football. Since coming here to Manchester United, I've seen supporters react with excitement and joy to the arrival of Eric Cantona from Leeds for about a million pounds, Andy Cole from Newcastle for seven million pounds, Jaap Stam for over ten million pounds, and Dwight Yorke for over twelve million pounds.

In these, and other similar cases, it seems to me that two

prerequisites were necessary for the transfer to take place. The first is a price: a price has to be agreed and paid between the selling club and the buying club. But even if a price is agreed, and all the documentation made out, the transfer only goes ahead when the player himself signs the documents. The selling club can sign and the buying club can sign, but the transaction will only proceed if there is a pledge by the player involved. His commitment, his signature, moves the transfer from the realm of potential to the realm of reality.

The Bible speaks of the reality of a spiritual transfer, which is made possible through the death and resurrection of Jesus Christ. In Colossians 1:13 we read, 'For he [that is, God] has rescued us from the dominion of darkness and brought us into the kingdom of the Son he loves, in whom we have redemption, the forgiveness of sins.' That verse talks about a huge spiritual transfer. Paul is telling Christians that Jesus Christ has transferred them from the dominion of darkness into the kingdom of the Son of God. The dominion of darkness means all that is against God, all that is opposed to the ways of God's kingdom, all that is under the power of sin, death and hell. Jesus has rescued us from that darkness and brought us into the kingdom of the Son of God in whom we find redemption and forgiveness. Redemption is a theological word that speaks of a price being paid in order for freedom to be bought. This great transfer brings to Christians freedom from all that sin and Satan can throw at us, and it brings mercy and forgiveness from God.

We noted that when a football transfer takes place, there are two prerequisites: one is the price which has to be paid, and the other is the pledge or commitment which the player has to make. So it is with the Christian transfer. A price has to be paid – and that price is the death of Jesus Christ, the Son of God. It was Jesus dying on a cross at Calvary, just outside Jerusalem, that makes it possible for you and I to know the reality of this great spiritual transfer. That is why the celebration and remembrance of that great event is central to all Christian denominations. Whether we call it the 'breaking of bread', or 'Eucharist', or 'Communion', or the 'Lord's Supper', or whatever, we remember the death of Jesus Christ that brings light and life to his people, and his grace and his mercy into our lives.

Yet this does not happen automatically. Just as a footballer is not immediately transferred when the buying and the selling sides have agreed their deal until he has given his own personal commitment, so are we involved in God's great spiritual transfer. We must be aware of exactly what we are committing ourselves to: that, however good we are, none of us is 100 per cent perfect, and we all need forgiveness; that we must turn from our way of life to God's way; that we really need to believe that Jesus died, so that we can be reached by God's mercy and forgiveness.

Once we come to understand all of that, we still need, to use the footballing analogy, to 'put our name on the contract'. We need to commit ourselves to receive all the benefits that Christ has won for us, and to give ourselves to him. For many Christians that point of commitment may come through the words of a simple prayer. It might be something like:

Father God, I realise that there are things in my life that are wrong, things in my life that do not please you. I am sorry for this and really want to turn away from living like that, and turn to living for you. I believe Jesus died to bring your love, forgiveness and power into my life. I ask you now to cleanse me from all wrong and sin that is part of me, and to make me new, and to send your Holy Spirit to me to bring your love and life and reality into my life. I promise, with your strength I will follow you for the rest of my days. Amen.

This is the great spiritual transfer, the great spiritual change of ownership and destiny, that is at the heart of Christian faith. It introduces us to a friendship, a relationship with Jesus Christ by the Spirit of God, and enables us to know the One who is Almighty God as our Father. Just like a football transfer, the spiritual transfer is the start of a new adventure, not the climax of it. It is a commitment that leads on to other things. A new manager must coach us, prepare us and integrate us into his squad, but we can be assured that ultimately we will receive a victory medal when the final whistle blows.

7

Managers, Trophies and Superstars

In this chapter we are developing the idea of sporting parables again as we consider Managers, Trophies and Superstars.

Managers

The role of the manager in a football club is as central as the role of a vicar or minister in a church. If the right person is appointed, then success, progress and growth can follow. However, a wrong appointment can bring difficulty and decline. Of course, there is much more to the life of a church than simply the minister or vicar, and much more to the life of a football club than the manager. Yet it seems to me that the correct appointment is absolutely vital for the success of any football club.

The manager, like the minister, is expected to be gifted and talented in many different areas. I remember helping out a church in the north of England that was going through a period without a full-time minister. I spoke to the lay leaders of the church about the sort of gifts and abilities that they wanted from the person they appointed. Did they have a job description? What particular strengths would be essential? What weaknesses could they tolerate? I found some very helpful material that tabulated potential areas of skill or strength for clergy, and as we went through this list together, it was helpful to hear the responses of the lay leadership. Yes, they wanted someone who would be a good Bible teacher because it was important to have a well-taught congregation. Yes, they wanted someone who would be excellent at leading worship because they wanted inspiring services, full of God's presence. Yes, they would want the new minister to be particularly gifted in evangelism, able to communicate the gospel to individuals, small groups and large gatherings. He would need to be gifted at relating to people outside the church, building bridges with the local community, a 'normal' person, not an overtly religious person. He would also have to be able to get on with people within the church: he would need to be particularly gifted at dealing with the youth because they have an important part to play in the life of the church, and, of course, he would also need to be very acceptable to the older people of the church, because they too are equally significant. He would need a capacity to relate well to other church leaders in the town, because they would not want their church to be isolated from the wider work and life of what God is doing in the area. He would need to be very gifted pastorally. He would be one who felt comfortable spending a regular time each week visiting church members in their homes, and offering pastoral advice and support to them and their families. He would need to be a good counsellor, one who listened well, and had experience and qualifications in counselling so that he could support members of the church in particular times of need or difficulty or trouble. Another essential quality would be his visionary ability. The church wanted someone who could think creatively, who was able to devise new strategies and ways forward. Indeed, it was essential that this individual was one who would inspire others. He would need to be a team player, who could enthuse and motivate both the ordinary members of the church and those with leadership responsibilities within it. He, therefore, would have to be well gifted in interpersonal skills, a 'people person'. The list continued as we considered other qualities. He would be a person with a strong personal devotional life. He would have a strong awareness of life in the real world. He would be expected to play a full and vibrant part in local and national denominational activities. He would be a trainer and equipper of various groups within the church. He would be committed to the idea of world mission, and would be able to take practical steps to inspire the church to a greater concern and involvement. He would be an organiser; he would be able to structure the life of the church so that its work would function to the optimum. He would be a really excellent administrator . . . So the list went on and on. We considered all of these qualities, and probably a few more, and I began to think that not even St Paul would have stood a chance of being shortlisted for the job. We laughed as someone pointed out that they might be waiting a long time before they actually discovered somebody who would be suited to taking on the job. We came to the conclusion that although there were many beneficial qualities that the potential minister might need, it was important for the church and the lay leaders to decide what were the three or four essential strengths that they were looking for.

All ministers are gifted in some areas, and are weaker or have limitations in others. If the congregation needs a Bible teacher to teach them the Scriptures and to feed them spiritually, but they end up appointing a pastor and a counsellor, then perhaps both the people and the minister will come to feel very frustrated, sometimes with disastrous results. The minister's job requires competence in many different areas of church work, but he must be *gifted* in those that the congregation particularly needs ministerial strength for at that time.

The job of a football manager is also varied and demanding, requiring skills in many contrasting areas of work. My mind goes back to the late 1970s and early 1980s when I was in a position to observe the job that Graham Taylor was doing at Watford Football Club. He seemed to be responsible for so many areas within this developing club. He was obviously responsible for coaching the first team and getting the results that were to take Watford from the Fourth Division through to Europe. He was also in charge of putting together a team of staff to coach the Reserves and beginning to nurture younger players who would be the foundation of the club's later success. In order to find suitable young talent he needed to establish a scouting system. He also sought to identify the location of a suitable training ground and complete appropriate negotiations that would secure such a facility for the club in the medium term. All of that was to do with the playing side of the club. Then there was the promotional and community sides to Graham's job, developing contacts with schools, hospitals, factories and local institutions, to raise the profile of the club in the community. This also provided some benefit to the playing side as well.

On one occasion I had asked Luther Blissett if he would be willing to visit a young person from our church, who was in Stanmore Orthopaedic Hospital. Mark had a problem with his spine which made it necessary for him to have some long, complex and dangerous surgery at Stanmore Orthopaedic Hospital. As the club trained at Stanmore, and as the boy in question was a huge fan of Luther Blissett, I asked Luther a little nervously if he would mind making a visit with me to cheer the lad up at a difficult time in his life. Luther, quite typically, was very willing to do that, but asked me to find a suitable date and check it out with the manager, which I did. Graham asked me to remind him a few days before the visit that Luther would be going to the hospital after training and to make the appropriate arrangements with the hospital ward. Everything was set up, and dutifully, two or three days before the date in question, I made contact with Graham to check that there was no problem. He decided to take the whole of the squad in, rather than simply let Luther visit on his own.

On the Thursday in question, when morning training was over, the players showered and changed into their official tracksuits, and went as a group to Stanmore Orthopaedic Hospital, to visit Mark and other children in similar circumstances on the ward. Graham told me afterwards that he'd done it, not only for Mark and the other sick children they visited, but also for the players, to help them get things in perspective. 'They are a bit down and disappointed that we have lost three games on the run,' he said. 'I wanted to show them that there are worse disasters in life than losing three football matches.' They saw children who had had some terrible accidents and had gone through some really traumatic operations. Some would be in hospital for six to ten weeks or more, and others were faced with the possibility of never being able to walk, or struggling, as indeed Mark was, with major spinal surgery. 'I wanted to put football matches into perspective,' he said. I know Mark and the staff at Stanmore Orthopaedic were absolutely thrilled at the results of the Watford players' visit, but I fancy Graham had also made his point. Two days later the team won their match. The manager also has to be a psychologist, and sometimes, it seemed, his concern to develop the club in the community and to raise its profile coincided with an opportunity to provide a positive psychological input for his players.

That capacity to motivate and inspire players is an essential quality in a football manager. Someone once said to me that the best way to judge a manager's motivational and inspirational abilities is to look at the difference between half-time score lines and full-time score lines. The manager has ten minutes with the players to motivate them for the situation they are facing in that individual game. The football club manager has to be an inspirer and motivator, but what is it that motivates the motivator? Is it ego? Is it thirst for personal success? Is it the fear of failure?

If we relate that to the situation of the Christian minister, what is it that motivates the person in full-time Christian service? I certainly hope it isn't ego, or thirst for success, or fear of failure. I believe Christian clergy need to be motivated by the Prime Motivator. We need to be people who can inspire and enthuse others, but not simply so that our church grows or our mission is successful. The bottom line for Christian motivation must be God: God's will, God's ways, God's purposes, and the growth of God's kingdom.

I find my present work with SCORE hugely demanding. Each year I travel between 20,000 and 25,000 miles, and there are many weeks when I work between sixty and eight hours. I hope the situation will change when we have the finance to employ other members of staff. Between 1995 and 2000, as SCORE was growing and the opportunities were increasing, I certainly found myself working too hard, constantly trying to put a quart into a pint bottle. I am motivated, not by ego, but by a sense that God is really involved in this particular work and ministry. I do what I do because of a sense of God's call, which has been confirmed in many ways, not least by other Christian leaders. I want to fulfil God's purposes. My personal choice would be to be a Bible teacher in a local church, but the call of God overrides my personal preference, motivating me in the ministry of God's choice. It is an awesome thought that while people in other professions may be self-motivated, Christians must be God-motivated. It is their experience of the love, truth, mercy and power of God that motivates their service and devotion for the growth of God's kingdom. We give our best to God, not out of fear of his power and might, but in response to his giving of his best to us. It is the motivation of committed love, the motivation of deep devotion.

I have already spoke about how my observation of Graham Taylor's involvement at Watford in those early days introduced me to the huge breadth of a manager's work. In addition to the wide range of responsibilities I have already described, I can remember Graham promoting the development of the stadium. He wanted to improve the administrative and organisational side of the club, and to that end brought in Eddie Plumley from Coventry City to oversee its smooth running.

He was concerned with Watford's commercial development and saw the need to restructure and to bring in suitable staff to further that process, his best signing in this area arguably being Caroline Gillies. Another of Graham's attributes was his ability to come over well in the media, whether it was in interviews with Oliver Philips, the local sports writer with the *Watford Observer* or via a growing number of TV interviews. Graham was good at communicating his vision for Watford as a developing family-orientated club with a close community involvement, which was also achieving success on the field.

What I saw at Watford through the 1980s I have seen again at Old Trafford in the 1990s: the role of an individual manager in bringing success to a football club. Sir Alex Ferguson's achievements as a football manager have made him a legend, not only in Manchester, but also across the UK, and particularly in Scotland. There they remember not only how he brought success to what is arguably the biggest club in England but also how he took Aberdeen to domestic and European glory. There can be no comparison between the Watford Football Club of the early 1980s and the Manchester United of the beginning of the twenty-first century: they are as different as chalk and cheese. The size and scope of the Old Trafford outfit means that the manager cannot act as the 'lord of the manor' to his club. He cannot be 'hands on' with other sectors of club life, but in Sir Alex I see a range of talent and ability that goes way beyond the coaching of a football team. I continue to be amazed by his energy, drive and commitment to the task. He is regularly found at the training ground at 7.30 a.m., and seems to find time to pack his day with a host of appointments, not all of which are essential to his work as manager of Manchester United Football Club. Many responsibilities come with that role, but on top of his managerial responsibilities and media requests he still finds time to respond positively to invitations which many others would simply turn down. He gives a lot of time to support and help people whom others might have no time for, or, at best, would ignore. His drive and enthusiasm combined with his knowledge, insights and motivational skills have clearly had a huge part to play in Manchester United's more recent successes. Where would the club be if Sir Alex had stayed with Aberdeen or gone elsewhere? Indeed, what would have happened to another club had he become their manager in the late 1980s?

The manager's influence is really vital. The right manager can turn a club round; he can bring success where there has been failure; he can bring hope where there has been despair. He can bring excellence where there has been mediocrity. This is another great footballing parable. Just as a football club needs the right manager to help it achieve its potential, so humanity, you and I, need a manager who can help us achieve the true potential of our lives. I really believe that Jesus Christ can have that impact on people today, just as he has had over hundreds of years of history. The message of the gospel of Jesus Christ, the powerful working in our lives of God, the Holy Spirit, and the creative impact of the teaching of Jesus Christ, and indeed, of the Christian Scriptures generally, provide for us as individuals a management package far more potent than even Alex Ferguson or Graham Taylor could ever devise. As individuals we find that God really is dealing with what is wrong and destructive and negative in our lives. It doesn't always happen instantly, and it is not always a painless process.

The Christian will find that the work of God's Spirit and the truth of God's Word, like the message of the gospel of Jesus, have a powerful potential to renew and recreate us. Time in the presence of God, open to his Word and open to his Spirit, is time spent in the presence of our supreme personal spiritual manager. God is able to change us and make us become more like the person he wants us to be. I believe without God as our manager we remain in our mediocrity. Our spiritual potential in Christ is never fulfilled. We continue to wallow around in our selfish state, separated from Christ and his love and power. A football manager may see great potential in a young player, even though his skills are not honed and he is raw and untutored. Just as that player can be coached by the manager and turned into someone who deserves a place in the team and who finds purpose and function through being a member of that team, so people can come under the management of Jesus Christ. The management that Jesus offers us begins with confession, repentance, faith and response, but must continue with discipleship, obedience and fellowship sprinkled with the challenge of sacrifice and the responsibility of Christian commitment. To have God as your manager is a wonderful privilege as well as a significant responsibility. We must live out the life, but we do so knowing God is with us. He will never leave us nor forsake us. His Spirit has come to dwell within our lives, and we are his people to the very end of the age, and indeed, beyond that. No football manager can make that commitment or that promise to any of his players, yet God not only sorts out our lives and brings us into his team, but also says that we are there, secure, for ever and for eternity.

Trophies

This brings us to the parable of football trophies. It was great to see some of Watford's success in those early years: Fourth Division Champions 1977–8, Third Division Champions 1978–9, promotion to Division One 1980–1, Runners-up Division One 1981–2, Cup Finalists 1983–4. The success of those years was remarkable for little Watford, but even more incredible is the success that Manchester United has achieved through the hard work of its manager, coaches and players in the 1990s.

I remember queuing up with my family and other members of staff to have our photograph taken with the Carling Premiership Trophy and the FA Cup following the 'Double Double' achieved in May 1996. This was, however, surpassed in December 1999, when again the family and I queued, with other members of staff, to have our photograph taken this time with four trophies: the Carling Premiership Trophy, the FA Cup, the Europe – South American Club Championship Trophy, and the most highly sought after and coveted trophy of all, the European Cup. Although there is an amazing uniqueness about some of these achievements, which we will never forget, they highlight a significant and challenging truth. Whatever a team wins in any one particular year has to be competed for again the following year if possession of that trophy is to continue. If you win the trophy, whether it is the Carling Premiership or the FA Cup or the European Cup, you retain it for a year and then lose it, unless you are able to win it again. The success of any particular year will be considered in future years and remembered with appreciation and with thankfulness, but the trophy won in 1968 is not there again in 1969. The memory of the 1968 achievement and its importance remains, but the fact is that the trophy is gone until it is won again, which it was by United in 1999.

While the sportsman or woman has to have the hunger to go out and win again, Christians know that they have been offered something that has been won once and for all. God offers to us the assurance of his love, his acceptance and his commitment to us which will last forever. St Paul makes this contrast when writing to the church in Corinth.

> Do you not know that in a race all the runners run, but only one gets the prize. Run in such a way as to get the prize. Everyone who competes in the games goes into strict training. They do it to get a crown that will not last; but we do it to get a crown that will last forever. (1 Corinthians 9:24–5)

Paul contrasts the temporary nature of the athlete's reward with the permanent nature of the Christian's reward. In our culture we can draw the same parallel from football. A team wins a championship one year, yet they have to go out and compete and win it again the next year. Their status as the champion of that year does not stretch into the following season when the championship has to be won again. However, those whom Christ has called champions are champions forever. Even when we don't feel like it, or when we don't deserve it, that title champion is still hung round our neck. When we feel too weak or too old to compete, and it is time to retire from the race that is 'life', then God still insists that we wear the insignia of champions. We leave this world clutching the trophy that he has given us *now*, which promises us a place with him, still hanging onto that trophy, in *eternity*.

In these days the Church has thought much about the excitement and the dynamic of the presence and the power of God within our lives. We tend to emphasise the God of the Now, how he impacts our present humanity, but we need to recapture an eternal perspective. We need to understand that there is a dimension to the Christian message that goes beyond our present experience of time and space. We believe in eternity, we believe in the hereafter, we believe in heaven, we believe in the resurrection of Jesus Christ which has provided a doorway for his people to walk through. We believe not just in a trophy for a season, but in a trophy that lasts forever.

Superstars

Four of five years ago, I was standing on what was then the forecourt in front of the East Stand at Old Trafford talking to one of the staff working in the area. It was summer holiday time and there were a good number of people about, with families visiting the Museum and Tour Centre, which was then located under a corner of that East Stand, and the Superstore. Cars were coming and going, so I didn't pay particular attention to a rather smart vehicle that had driven in and parked opposite the Superstore, maybe sixty or seventy metres away from the Reception Area at Old Trafford. A door slammed to, and there was the now familiar bleep of car locks and security systems becoming operative, before an individual strode across the forecourt to the Reception Area. It is perhaps appropriate that I can't remember who that individual was (it was either the Manager or one of our top young international players), but I remember the incident because of what happened in the next five or ten seconds. In the time that it took to walk the sixty metres from the parked car to the reception, an excited crowd of people had thronged around this individual. It was like a swarm of bees. Cameras were flashing, autograph books were being thrust out in front of the celebrity, questions were being asked, and names were being shouted. It had begun with three or four people recognising him as he got out of his car, and running towards him. Then one or two others, seeing the figures running, had also started to run. There were shouts of: 'Over here' and 'There's so-and-so', and in no time it seemed he was being mobbed by forty or fifty people.

My mind went back to the end of November 1977. At my first Monday-morning visit to Watford's training session at the YMCA, Graham Taylor had asked me to meet him at the ground some time between 9.30 and 9.45 a.m. so that we could walk up together. As we walked along we talked about a whole range of topics. I think, actually, Graham talked and I listened. I found him a man full of interesting opinions and ideas, and I always enjoyed talking to him at some depth. That morning we talked about fame. Graham made the point that fame may seem to bring great benefits, but it also comes with a great cost. As the Elton John and Bernie Taupin tribute to Marilyn Monroe, the song *Candle in the Wind*, says: 'Hollywood made you a Superstar, Fame was the price you paid'. I remember him saying: 'You and I can go into Marks & Spencers and buy underwear or socks, a pair of trousers or a shirt, and do so in relative anonymity but our Chairman can't do any of that. He can't walk down a street, go into a store and do normal shopping. He's not able to do that. He's rich and he's famous, but he hasn't got the sort of privacy that you and I would enjoy.' Sadly, twenty years later, Graham would be able to talk more meaningfully about the cost of fame and a high public profile.

In the late 1970s my links with Watford Football Club had given me the opportunity to get to know one or two people from the playing or coaching side of football who had expressed their Christian convictions publicly. One of those was a Scotsman who played for Swindon Town as goalkeeper, Jimmy Allen. Swindon, at that time, was not a particularly high flying club, and Jimmy would have regarded himself as just an ordinary player earning a living at an ordinary club in what was then either Division Two or Three of the English League. I remember Jimmy saying to me that, although he may not be famous on an English or Scottish stage, in Swindon he was known, and in his locality there was huge interest in anything that he, or the other players at the club, was involved in. He told me about an occasion when he went to a local school to speak at their Christian Union about his life in football and the importance of his Christian faith. He said normally they would get ten or fifteen lads to their Christian Union meeting, but on this occasion they publicised it 'Jimmy Allen, goalkeeper at Swindon Town Football Club', and they got nearly 350 or 400 attending. The meeting had to be moved from the classroom that was used for RE to the school hall, so that the crowds could be accommodated. He was making the point that the interest was generated not because of the name Jimmy Allen, but because it was Jimmy Allen, goalkeeper of Swindon Town Football Club. The boys came to hear someone they regarded as a sports personality, a star in their locality. If it had been Jimmy Allen, civil servant working at Swindon Town Hall, then maybe there would have been ten or fifteen people there as normal, but

Jimmy Allen, goalkeeper, Swindon Town Football Club player, brought more than half the school to the assembly hall that lunchtime. In the eyes of many the footballer is a star – even if he doesn't play in the top division, even if he's associated with a lesser club, he's still given hero status in his locality.

As a teenager Matt Tees, a Scottish striker signed by Grimsby Town from Airdrie, was one of my great footballing heroes. I didn't join in the chants of 'Matt, Matt, Matt' that echoed round Blundell Park verbally, but I was joining in on the inside, and I remember being very hurt once when a fan from the opposing club standing next to me asked me: 'Do you call him Matt because he spends so much time on the ground?' This was after he had noticed another appeal for a foul in the penalty box.

Our local heroes, however, face nothing of the pressure that is now experienced by some of the superstars from the top clubs. It is for that reason that as chaplain to Manchester United Football Club I would never seek autographs or tickets or favours from players. Well, *never* is not absolutely accurate. I can remember one occasion when a charity asked me if I could get a bottle of whisky autographed by the Manchester United players. It was a good cause but I was reluctant as chaplain to compromise my relationship with the players and I didn't want to add to their harassment. I explained my dilemma to Brian Kidd, who was at that time the Assistant Manager. Brian's comment was that they knew me well enough and knew that I was genuine, and they would do it for me if I asked them to. I followed his advice and the players were helpful and obliging. However, I look back at that incident with some regret. Although I was able to help a very good cause, I was sorry to have broken my golden rule never to ask for autographs. I haven't done it since. I think, as a general rule, chaplains should not use their privileged position to put more pressure on players by asking for autographs or other favours.

In our SCORE training sessions with chaplains we always try to stress that the chaplain is not there to take from the club, but to give to it. There should always be demonstrably more put in by the chaplain than is taken out. We would certainly warn them against seeking autographs or other favours from the superstars at their clubs. This rule can lead to disappointment, particularly to the young fans I meet as I travel the country. Maybe two weekends a month I am involved in events organised by a local church from Friday to Sunday evening. Usually, at some stage over such a weekend, a young fan of Manchester United will come up, normally very politely, and ask if it would be possible for me to get the autographs of such-and-such a player. I have to explain that he can write to the club to ask, but I'm not in a position to act as a go-between. I don't do it for myself, I don't do it for my own children, and I feel it's not fair for me to do it for people around the country. If I did it for one, I'd have to do it for everybody. I hope people understand the reasoning behind this. I certainly wouldn't want to add to the pressures that the top footballers face.

I would add that many of the players I have worked alongside, both at Watford and at Manchester United, are well aware that their involvement with football brings not only privileges but also responsibilities. I remember one training session at the Cliff training ground during the school holidays in 1996 or 1997. A huge crowd of young school children had invaded the area at the Cliff, where players parked their cars.

Frank, Harold and the other stewards were having a really tough job monitoring the crowds, but did their best with their normal joviality. The children were waiting for people like Eric Cantona, Ryan Giggs, David Beckham and others in the first team squad. I remember those three particular players coming out and, starting at one end of this huge line of fans, simply walking down the line signing one autograph after another. It must have taken the best part of an hour, but they did it because of their commitment to the fans who support them. One of the car park attendants commented that this was particularly typical of Eric Cantona. If possible, he always waited until the last request was made for an autograph before driving off, whether it was at the Cliff training ground or at Old Trafford, or even after a game. Perhaps that was one of the reasons why he was regarded by so many fans as such a hero.

I quite enjoy listening to debates on TV or radio where a group of pundits express their opinions about the best player or the most valued player or the most perfect player in a particular team, or season, or even country. Fans or journalists may consider many different aspects of a player's game: his general ability to influence a game, his ball control, his passing skills, his tackling and creativity in finding space, his ability to score goals or defend, his coolness under pressure, his temperament. They judge, too, whether his performance is consistent rather than patchy and whether there is a significant impact on the team when he is not able to play. All these factors are added to the melting pot. The truth is that no player is one hundred per cent perfect; there may be a weakness of pace, in the air or on the ground, in temperament or goal scoring, in defending or attacking. Every player will display flaws. True, the better the player the less flaws there will be but no one can put in a one hundred per cent performance all the time. The search for an absolutely perfect superstar will always be quite frustrating. There are many great, enormously talented players but none of them plays an absolutely perfect game all of the time. Because they are human there will always be the occasional misplaced pass or mistimed tackle, or a shot that is off target.

This is a concept I have used to illustrate the message of the Christian gospel – another football parable. The point of the life, death and resurrection of Jesus Christ is not that you've got to be really good and try really hard so that God will accept you and give you a ticket to heaven. The gospel is for those who know they are not good enough, who know they are morally weak, who know that they fail and need forgiveness. For such people the Christian gospel brings hope.

One of the key Bible verses that helps us understand our state before God is: 'For all have sinned and fall short of the glory of God' (Romans 3:23). God's glory is his holiness, his purity, his goodness, his justice, his love. God is absolutely perfect: one hundred per cent. But every single human being falls short of that. Sin is part of our character. I don't believe that this means that every aspect of our being is wrong and evil all the time, but it does mean that our whole character is tainted: we are less than perfect. We all do things, think things and say things that are wrong. We all fail our own standards, let alone God's. That is why the Christian faith is so relevant to all of us, because it deals with human nature as it really is. A Christian message about forgiveness, cleansing, a fresh start becomes enormously relevant.

There is a second major theme that I would like to explore

under this heading of superstars, and that is the issue of transience and lasting significance. As I have mentioned, my boyhood hero was Matt Tees. However, a visit to Grimsby Town Football Club today will confirm that the days of Matt Tees are over. He was a great player in his day and made a wonderful contribution to the club, but now his playing career is finished; he is consigned to history. He is appreciated, looked back on with affection, and there are many happy memories, but his direct relevance is over.

It is the same at Watford and Manchester United. The Vicarage Road heroes of the late 1970s and 1980s – men like Steve Sherwood, Roger Joslyn, Dennis Booth, Ian Bolton, Steve Sims, Nigel Callaghan, John Barnes, Ross Jenkins – are remembered with great esteem and affection, at least by Watford fans. Their memory lingers, but their influence is gone. They belong to a past era. This came home to me again when I was watching one of the videos of Manchester United's success in the early 1990s. There were players in the Double winning side of 1993–4 that were regarded as awesome heroes by the fans of that season. Think of Bryan Robson, Steve Bruce, Gary Pallister, Andrei Kanchelskis, Lee Sharpe, Paul Ince, Brian McClair, Mark Hughes and Eric Cantona. Each in their own way was a wonderful player and each played a significant part in that season's remarkable success – yet now they are gone. Their memory lives on, and their achievement is regarded with huge esteem and affection, but as people they no longer have any influence over Manchester United's fortunes on the field. As players, their time has gone; their influence is ended.

In contrast with these football heroes stands one whose life continues to influence millions throughout the world. If ever there was a hero then it was Jesus Christ. If ever there was a superstar, it was Jesus Christ. Yet he had none of the trappings that would go with the title and none of his human attributes would suggest superstardom.

Born in a humble Middle Eastern home, living a very basic life, untutored, yet teaching the world, a victim of concerted opposition yet victorious in it all, Jesus Christ answers the deepest needs of humanity. Accomplishing more through his dying than through his living, uniquely he still lives today. Jesus Christ, Christians believe, is God in human form. Many come to know him as there Saviour and Lord, bringing the love, grace, forgiveness and power of God into their lives. He is the One who illuminates their darkness. He is the One who replaces despair with hope. He is the One who, in the present, assures us of a future. It is Jesus Christ who confirms that we are with God now and will be with him throughout eternity. It is his lasting influence that contrasts with the transience of our football heroes. Their influence lasts for a number of seasons, perhaps a decade at the most, and then they retire. The game says, 'Thank you, but we don't want you any more.' The relevance of Jesus Christ goes on and on and on.

8

Memorable Meetings

I have already explained why it is not appropriate for me as a chaplain to sports people to write an exposé of some of the more interesting or juicier conversations that I have been involved in, but I hope it will be helpful to write about some of the individuals whose Christian experience and faith is particularly significant to them. As I do, I want to affirm that the Christian message is relevant both to the successful and the unsuccessful, the star player and the most inexperienced office junior. Joining the Church is not like joining a club or a particular interest group. The Christian Church is made up of people whose lives have been changed by their becoming believers in, and followers of, Jesus Christ. They all have a relationship with God through Jesus Christ. As we have already seen, part of the outworking of that relationship might be church services and Christian activity.

Church may or may not be helpful as individuals begin to think about issues relating to spirituality and eternity, personal significance, the existence of God or what may happen to us when we die. The truth is that while there are some churches that convey very effectively the truth, reality and relevance of the Christian message, there are others which do not. That is very sad indeed.

The Christian message is relevant to all sectors of our society. The size of your house, the make of your car (or shoes!), the strength of your bank balance (or the size of your overdraft!) and the design of your clothes are all peripheral to the key spiritual questions of life. Yet some people feel that, if only they were famous, if only they had riches and wealth, if only they had made their mark on society in a big way, then they would have peace and satisfaction. But the experiences of life tells us that this is not so. You buy your own flat and are wonderfully happy moving into it, and yet after a little while feel you need to move to a little semi. You are happy in that for a little while, but then see the need to move perhaps to a bigger semi, and then to a larger detached house and then one larger still, perhaps with a double garage and a more extensive garden. The society we live in encourages us to be unsatisfied with what we have. People are always seeking more. You may long for a new car; for a while it's only a dream but eventually you have the possibility of purchasing your new model. You are happy with it for a year or two, but then it is no longer a new model, and you feel an urge to buy something bigger and better and newer. The same can apply in relationships. After a little while you may feel that a new model would suit your circumstances better there also.

I contend that it is a mistaken belief that says 'Our personal contentment, our personal sense of purpose and direction and our inner peace will come about solely because of the materialism that we surround ourselves with.' I agree that it is possible to be more economically comfortable if we have the material things we need, but that is not the same as an inner personal peace. That comes from God and from knowing God's love for us.

The office junior and the superstar are both confronted with the spiritual questions of life. Many will seek to ignore them, but some will acknowledge their relevance and their reality. Some will acknowledge that the issues of guilt and forgiveness are very real. Some will acknowledge that the issues of inner peace and purpose are significant. Some will acknowledge that our life on earth will, at some time in the future, come to an end, confronting us with the question of what is beyond it all. I hope too that everyone will be confronted with the truth that Christians are real people. That they are not odd, they are not freakish and they are not 'out of touch with reality', but that there is a genuineness about their lifestyle that says: 'We have found something'.

What I hope Christian people convey is not simply the relevance of the spiritual dimension, not simply some vague, ethereal spirituality about a God somewhere or spiritual forces or 'something beyond ourselves'. I hope Christian people convey something of the person and the truth of Jesus Christ and the power and the work of the Holy Spirit, who is God at work in our lives.

I am very traditional and biblical in my Christian belief. I am Trinitarian in doctrine, and would wish to be Christo-centric in declaration. I believe in one God who is Father, Son and Holy Spirit and I believe in one mediator between a sinful humanity and God who is holy beyond compare, that is Jesus Christ. I believe that he lived on earth as the incarnate Son of

God, and that he was crucified under Pilate, buried and raised again to life eternal. I believe his death is an atoning sacrifice for the sins of mankind, and that individually we can come to know the love, grace and truth of God as we respond to Jesus Christ and the message of his Gospel. I believe those who come into his Kingdom, who come to experience the love of God in Christ in their own lives, have got a message to share with the world. This is not simply a message from a book or the teachings from a pulpit, but also from their own experience. One of my favourite illustrations is to consider how something as simple as chickenpox can help us understand the depth and the power of the Christian message. We can learn about chickenpox from a book, a medical book that teaches us its incubation period, symptoms and virulence, and how it is caught and passed on. We can learn more about chickenpox by talking to someone who has actually had the disease. They might remember how they first noticed it appearing and reflect on how they caught it. They would certainly tell us the symptoms and what it is like, and the impact it has had on their lives. There may even be a few spots and blotches on their skin that remind them of the disease. But the best way to learn about chickenpox would be to actually catch it ourselves. Christian faith can be experienced in the same way. We can learn about it from a book, we can see it in the lives of others, but ultimately, if we are to experience the fullness of it, we need to experience it personally for ourselves.

Another illustration that helps to indicate the difference between theological theory and personal reality is an old and often used one. About a hundred years ago Blondin, the French tightrope walker, was engaging in remarkable high wire feats in Europe and the USA. On one occasion a high wire was rigged across the Niagara Falls for Blondin to walk across. Crowds had gathered to see him and applauded as, holding a balancing pole, he walked first one way and then back again. They were enraptured by his talent and bravery. Blondin then took a wheelbarrow and explained that he would push this wheel-barrow across the wire while someone sat in it. The crowd applauded enormously and shouted 'Bravo!' to him. When Blondin asked the gathered throng if they thought this was possible, they cheered affirmingly. Blondin then looked at them and said, 'Who will come and sit in the wheelbarrow?' There was silence. Although everyone believed that Blondin could do the great feat, no one actually wanted to express their personal trust in him by sitting in the wheelbarrow. They believed in their mind that the feat was possible, but they were not willing to take a step of faith.

As I have explained, my beliefs are normal, traditional, biblical, Christian beliefs, but there is more to a living faith than just having beliefs. As the Blondin illustration points out, it is possible to believe something in our heads without it having any impact on our lives. But faith is belief in action. Faith says: 'This I believe and I respond to that belief, and my call is not simply that people understand the beliefs of Christianity, but that they are helped to take their own steps of faith, which is faith in Jesus Christ.'

For some people that faith can come in a remarkable, instantaneous conversion, but for most it is a slower and more gradual process. We need to understand both what the basic message about Jesus is saying, and how we can respond to it. I trust that what you have read in this book will help you do that. I also hope that the following brief stories of people that I have met in the football world will show you how Christian faith has changed some people's lives.

Alan West

I have already referred to Alan West as the player who, as Luton Town captain, opened my eyes to the possibility of chaplaincy work in football, and also gave me positive encouragement fifteen years later to respond to the invitation from Manchester United Football Club. But Alan has not always been a religious sort of individual.

He joined Burnley Football Club as an apprentice professional, and progressed well with them, representing England at under-21 level before being the transfer target of Sunderland FC in the early 1970s. His medical, prior to the signing of the forms that would seal the £100,000 transfer, raised questions about a possible back injury and Sunderland Football Club decided to pull out of the transfer. It was then, a week or two later, that Luton Town stepped in, and, having made their own medical assessment, declared that Alan was fit and well and could be signed at minimal risk. He became an established play-maker on the left side of Luton's midfield and a good passer of the ball, and his career progressed well. Two or three years later his life was to change dramatically. Alan and Cathy, his wife, went to visit Cathy's parents in New Zealand. Although they did not have a Christian background, they had become Christians in New Zealand and were very involved in a local church. Alan and Cathy were overwhelmed by the love, concern and welcome shown by members of that local church. At first they were puzzled at the changes they had seen in the lives of Cathy's mum and dad, but, by the time they returned to England after their holiday, both Cathy and Alan had become Christians. They had realised that there was something significantly different about Cathy's parents and had begun to investigate what this 'Christian thing' was all about. Alan returned to England a very different man.

People soon noticed that there was something different about him, and within a week or two questions were being asked that he began to answer. The news spread that 'Westy had got religion'. A local reporter got hold of the story and did a major interview with Alan, who simply told it as it was. That story appeared in the local press, and now everybody knew about Alan West's new-found faith in Christ. Alan served Luton admirably as a player, as the club captain and as a wonderful ambassador for the club in its community. When he left the club to join Millwall, the then manager, David Pleat, publicly gave a glowing tribute to Alan West, describing him as one of the finest professional footballers he had ever worked with: dedicated, honest, responsible and highly committed. His brief spell at Millwall ended when the manager at that time, George Graham, confronted him with the stark reality that his legs had gone (for those not too conversant with football, this is a footballers' term, meaning 'You can't run like you used to' – there was no question of Westy having his legs amputated or anything like that!) For a brief spell Alan left Millwall to be player/manager at Hitchin Town, but he then began to train for ministry in the church that he had made his home way back in the mid 1970s, Luton Christian Fellowship, part of the Elim Pentecostal denomination. He is still the Senior Minister and the leader of the ministry team of this growing and dynamic church. We, in SCORE, have appreciated the church's support in many ways. They have been keen to pray for our ministry, to give donations to our work and make their premises available to us for occasional trustees' meetings when we need a venue in the south of England. Alan continues to be supportive and helpful in his role as a member of SCORE's Board of Reference.

Alan's story reminds us of two truths. First, the impact of Christian care and compassion transparently lived out in front of other people cannot be overestimated. It was not so much what the church and family in New Zealand said, but what they *did* that made an impact on Alan and Cathy West. Second, we should note that here was a couple with no particular Christian background who suddenly found in Christian faith answers to their personal emptiness. Alan and Cathy will tell you that they were a couple whose lives were full of football, fame and parties, and yet there was a clear sense of personal emptiness. The faith in Jesus Christ they found in New Zealand not only survived the long journey back and Alan's involvement in professional football in England, but has continued right up to this present day despite the trials and tribulations that life brings. While still in her forties, Cathy needed hip replacement surgery after struggling for two years with the pain and anguish of a degenerating hip joint. Yet through that pain the Christian vitality of Cathy and Alan West shone like a beacon in the darkness. Their lives and their lifestyle speak of the reality of Jesus Christ and affirm the power of his message of love, grace and forgiveness. The West family, Alan and Cathy and their boys Ben and Josh, stand as witnesses to Christian truth. Alan's story says that, in the midst of the glitz and the bubble, and sometimes the pain and anguish, of the professional footballer's life, there is something of profound significance to be found which can fill the emptiness and bring to life its true perspective. That something is a real and vibrant faith in Jesus Christ.

Dennis Bailey

The second person I would like to introduce you to is Dennis Bailey. I got to know Dennis as a young player who had an extended trial at Watford Football Club when he was sixteen or seventeen. After several months of training with the under-eighteen squad and playing in the Saturday morning Junior League – the South East Counties League – Dennis was eventually released. He was taken on by Crystal Palace and began to make a name for himself there in the reserves and in the first team. He eventually moved on to Queens Park Rangers and latterly to Gillingham and Lincoln. It was probably with Queens Park Rangers that Dennis achieved his greatest success. On New Years Day 1992 he was a member of the QPR squad to play the then First Division leaders at Old Trafford. Remarkably, Queens Park Rangers won 3–1, and it was Dennis Bailey who scored a miraculous hat trick. At the press conference he spoke of his delight, but also of his faith in God. That message appeared on the back of most newspapers the next day.

Dennis's family had been churchgoing, but Christian faith only became real to him when, at the age of seventeen, he went to Loftus Road, the Queens Park Rangers' ground, not to play football this time but to listen to the South American evangelist, Luis Palau. Dennis responded to the appeal at the end of the message by going forward and giving his life to Christ. By this time he had left Watford, but someone told me that an ex-Watford player had made a Christian commitment at the Luis Palau meeting at Queens Park Rangers Football Club. I discovered it was Dennis and I wrote to him, sending him some booklets that I hoped would be helpful, and encouraged him to get involved with a church.

Our paths have crossed many times since, not least on the occasion in the spring of 1992 when Dennis agreed to be the guest speaker at the Watford Football Club Centenary Service in St Mary's Parish Church. I had organised the Centenary Service as part of a series of celebrations to mark that great landmark. It was quite appropriate that the service should be held in St Mary's Parish Church. Like many football clubs, Watford's origins, at least in part, have church connections. In the late 1800s Watford St Mary's were a significant football force in south-west Hertfordshire. It was their amalgamation with another football team that brought Watford Football Club into being. Various personalities were involved in that service, in which we gave thanks to God for a hundred years that had brought a sporting focus to the town and enjoyment to some of its people. Dennis was the ideal speaker to bridge the gap between Christian Church and professional football. He came back to us as one who had started out at the club, who had experienced some of the ups and downs of life at Vicarage Road, and as someone who in the contemporary world could speak about the significance and importance of Christian faith.

Dennis's playing career is coming to an end, but the importance of his faith continues. He certainly only occasionally hit the national headlines as a footballer, but once he had made his Christian commitment he was determined to honour God by the way he played his football. He was once asked why, when he was chasing through defenders in the penalty box at pace, he didn't go down when they came close to him in an attempt to win a penalty for his team and help them gain an advantage. He replied that that wasn't the way he played football. He wanted to be honest and truthful. Cheating and diving wasn't for him, and if he ever went down in the area it would be because of a defender genuinely causing him to trip or to overbalance. Dennis has always wanted his faith to be seen in his working life, and that's a great lesson we can learn from his story.

Perhaps there is an even more significant lesson which goes back to his Christian foundations. While it was members of his family who encouraged him to go to church and to make God part of his life, Dennis came to realise that his faith could not be second-hand. It wasn't sufficient for him simply to rely on the faith of others: that faith needed to be exercised and activated by him personally. The challenge of Luis Palau at Queens Park Rangers led Dennis to his own personal Christian commitment. This step of faith opened the door to a Christian life and lifestyle, not because he was following a pattern imposed by his family, but because it was something he had discovered for himself. Dennis's faith might owe much to his family background and to their encouragement and prayers, but it's a very personal and real faith, which he now pursues with commitment and devotion.

Cyrille Regis

The guest speaker at the Celebration Dinner of the 1998 SCORE Football Chaplains' Conference at the National Sport and Recreation Centre in Shropshire was the West Bromwich Albion coach, Cyrille Regis. His story was inspirational.

Cyrille had started out with the non-league club of Hendon before moving to West Bromwich Albion where he embarked on a career in professional football. His impressive progress led him to representative honours with the England under-21 B squad and then full international level. He was enjoying his football, with success on the pitch and a playboy lifestyle off the pitch, when a tragedy rocked his life.

Cyrille's close friend, Laurie Cunningham, was killed in a car crash in Spain. Laurie was a flying winger with West Brom who had gone on to play for Real Madrid in Spain. The two friends had kept in contact and Cyrille would sometimes visit Laurie. On one occasion, after a somewhat wild party, they were involved in a car crash while driving home, but both of them got out alive. The consequences of a second car crash, a couple of years later, were, however, tragic. Laurie was killed.

The fact that the circumstances of the accident were so similar to the first situation – another late night, another drive home – had a huge impact on Cyrille. He began to wonder why, two years earlier, he had escaped, and yet now Laurie had been killed. He began to wonder whether the life of a superstar footballer was all that great after all. Popularity, fame, invitations to parties, fast cars and fast women seemed very attractive, but the consequence of that lifestyle was the death of his best friend. Cyrille began to ask questions. What is life all about? What happens after we die? He knew he could so easily have been killed in that car with Laurie.

Cyrille found a Christian who was willing to talk to him and began to think through some of his questions. To cut a long story short, it was through those conversations that Cyrille came to realise what the Christian faith is all about and to make his own personal step of faith in Jesus Christ.

Cyrille's faith has been there for all to see through his remaining days at West Bromwich Albion, through his time at Coventry City and on through Aston Villa and then a series of other clubs. Eventually his career brought him back to West Brom where he is now a respected coach. He doesn't claim to be perfect, but he knows the forgiveness, love and power of Jesus Christ and seeks to serve him as he works in the world of professional football.

Cyrille's story focuses our attention on a couple of issues. Here is a man at the height of his career in professional football; he is a hero and legend at a club where the supporters love him. He is doing well financially, he seems to be enjoying a wonderful lifestyle and he has achieved success with both his club and his country. If we went to any twelve- or thirteen-year-old boy and asked him what he would like to do in life, what success would mean for him, many would say that by the age of twenty-five or twenty-six they wanted to be a footballing hero in the top division, to play for their country, and to enjoy all the fame and adulation that football can bring. Many people would aspire to that dream. Many people would give anything to have been Cyrille Regis in May 1987 when Coventry beat Spurs in the Cup Final at Wembley. Cyrille had found sporting success, but the truth is that sporting success does not answer the deep questions of life and death and eternity. Sporting success might be good for you emotionally, and it might do wonders for your social life, but it doesn't deal with the spiritual dimension that is part of our being. We see, in the story of Cyrille Regis, that there are issues and questions that can only be answered from a spiritual perspective.

The other lesson that we learn from Cyrille's story is the role of tragedy in bringing us to our senses. When all is well many people do not ever contemplate the deep questions of life. Yet I have found in my experience that when tragedy and disaster come close, then people are prompted to think more seriously about spiritual issues. It might be a family bereavement, a health scare, a financial crisis, unemployment or a national catastrophe. Around the time of the Munich

Memorial Service, forty years after the air crash in 1958, I remember speaking to one of our younger players. He, like many, had watched local TV programmes about those 'Busby Babes' and the tragic events at Munich Airport, and he said to me: 'You know, Rev., it makes you think: they were just like us now, they were young lads. They'd grown up together, they thought the whole of life was before them. They were doing well, and they were expecting to do better. They were enjoying success and they were enjoying football, and then suddenly it's all gone. In an instant it's all over. It begins to make you think, doesn't it Rev.? It really does make you think.'

Perhaps death, more than anything else, confronts us with the truth about life. How do we cope with that ultimate and final reality? Do we pretend it's not there, that it won't come to us, and try to blot it out of our mind? Do we react with anger, accusing God of being unjust in giving us such a transient life that at times seems so painful and unfair? Or do we react as Cyrille Regis reacted? He had lost a close friend, Laurie, who had died long before his time. Laurie was a man who was enjoying life, who was talented and good to be with, and then he was no more. But instead of reacting negatively, Cyrille reacted positively.

Either life has no meaning and we are here for an instant and then we are gone, in which case 'Eat, drink and be merry, for tomorrow we die' could be the philosophy for us all. Or we can take a more mature and philosophical view that says, 'Surely there must be more to life than that. Surely, if life is followed by death and death comes to us all, then if there is meaning in life there must be meaning beyond life. If there is meaning beyond life, then what are the answers to the questions about eternity and life beyond death?'

Cyrille began to explore the Christian answers to the questions of life and death and he came, not simply, to find an answer that his mind found satisfactory, but he made a discovery that has revolutionised his whole being. His spiritual life has 'come alive' as God began to work in response to his prayer of commitment to Christ. In extreme tragedy Cyrille Regis found peace, love, truth and the reality of God, but we don't have to wait for tragedy to come before we find those things.

Gavin Peacock

Another Christian footballer I have bumped into from time to time is Gavin Peacock, who began his career at Gillingham before moving on to Bournemouth and then on to the Premiership stage at Newcastle and Chelsea before signing for Queens Park Rangers. I had met Gavin in the course of my visits to chaplains at other clubs, but also when his team Chelsea played at Old Trafford. He always seemed to do particularly well against Manchester United and had an excellent scoring record against us, which was quite frustrating. As a fellow Christian I would often greet him and say, 'I hope you do well, God bless you,' but I really didn't want God to bless him that much, or for him to do that well. He always seemed to steal a winning goal against us.

Gavin grew up in a footballing family. I've met his father, Keith, at Charlton Athletic where he has been on the coaching staff for several years, having returned to the club where he was once a player. If we can reason that it was Keith Peacock who was responsible for son Gavin's football skills and interests, we can conclude that his mum was primarily responsible for the spiritual side of Gavin's life. He was not particularly a churchgoing lad, but he noticed a very significant change in his mother's life. She had started to go to church again, and it wasn't just what she did on Sunday that was beginning to impress Gavin. He noticed that she seemed to be altogether different as a person – not just on Sunday, but throughout the week. She was more at peace with herself, and with the world, and seemed to have found 'something', or, as Gavin was to find out, 'someone' who had made a major difference to her life. It was a difference that Gavin wanted to investigate for himself, and so he, too, started to go to church to find out what this Christian faith was all about.

When Gavin became a Christian, one of the things that excited him most was a sense of God with him. God was no longer a remote entity way up there in the sky somewhere, but was someone who he knew was living within his heart and spirit, someone who was with him and within him and around him. He could talk to God. God was there as someone with whom he could share the ups and downs of life. The full details of Gavin's spiritual pilgrimage have been recorded in books and on video, and are well worth reading, or watching. His story has so much to teach us. Perhaps the most significant aspect of his story is the fact that his Christian faith really puts his life in perspective. For a sportsman, particularly, life can be full of ups and downs: one week you are a hero, the next week you're a villain. One week you've done something awesome and marvellous, and you receive the adulation of thousands; the next week something negative has happened, and the fans mock you and ridicule you. Life outside sport can be full of ups and downs too. Gavin has found, like so many other Christians, that life with Jesus Christ provides a friendship to lift us up when we're down, and to put elation and success in meaningful perspective.

Both on and off the field, Gavin has had to cope with some great successes and some deep disappointments, but his Christian faith, his friendship with Jesus Christ, is the stabilising factor in his life, more than anything else is. One of my personal recollections of Gavin was when he played for Chelsea in the 1994 FA Cup Final. Anne and I had been invited to go with the staff on their day out at Wembley, and, of course, we very much wanted United to win. 'The Double' was on. I was very much hoping that the Manager, his staff and players would receive just reward for their great efforts that year. I was aware, though, that my Christian brother was playing for Chelsea. I did pray for him that day, that he would know the peace and presence of God as he played in this important game, and I prayed that God would strengthen him to play and act in a way that was good, right and honourable.

Before United scored their opening goal there was a brilliant piece of skill from Gavin, and a chipped shot clipped the top of the bar but didn't go in. On that great stage he failed to hit the target, but on the stage of life he's definitely 'on target'. His fellow professionals know there is something special about Gavin; they know that his Christian faith gives him a sense of peace and perspective which so many others find is lacking. But it needn't be, because that faith can be theirs and it can be yours as well.

Phil Starbuck

Phil Starbuck was a guest speaker at the 1999 Football Chaplains' Conference organised by SCORE, sponsored by the FA Carling Premier League, and held at the National Sport and Recreation Centre at Lilleshall. He was one of several speakers, because, as usual, we wished to provide a mix of teaching and training, spiritual meat and inspiration, and also a consideration of issues and trends within the football world. All this would help clergy working in that environment. We were delighted that Phil Starbuck was able to join us, because he has an active knowledge of both the football side and the Christian side.

I've met Phil on several occasions, but one of the most memorable was at Leeds United's Elland Road ground. It was in the 1992–3 season, and I had been invited some months earlier by their chaplain, Steve Riley, to speak at a men's dinner event organised by Steve's church. I'd agreed to come and it was booked into my diary five or six months in advance. Interestingly, on the Monday or Tuesday before the Sunday evening when I was due to speak at Elland Road, Manchester United had signed Eric Cantona from Leeds. There's generally no love lost between Leeds United and Manchester United supporters, and I knew that the signing of Cantona would add a little spice to my visit that Sunday evening. Steve, first of all, introduced Phil Starbuck, who spoke well and powerfully about his coming to faith and the way that the person of Jesus Christ continues to be a significant influence on his day-to-day life and lifestyle. It was great stuff to listen to and I felt quite inspired as he sat down and Steve Riley got up to introduce me. He said something like, 'I want to introduce a good friend of mine. John has been involved in football club chaplaincy since 1977, and has been a help to me as I've worked here at Leeds United. I'm delighted that he's able to share with us some of his insights on sport and on life. He's currently the chaplain at Manchester United Football Club, and I'd like you to give a warm Leeds welcome to the Revd

John Boyers.' As I stood up and Steve Riley sat down, it seemed as though 120 Yorkshiremen booed as to a man. I conveyed warm Christian greetings from my home church, Altrincham Baptist, and warm footballing salutations from Manchester United Football Club. That didn't go down terribly well at Elland Road, but when I told them that deep down I was a Grimsby Town fan there was a little laughter and some sympathy. After the presentation Phil and I had a chance to talk about our respective involvements in football. He was then a player at Sheffield United Football Club.

Two significant events in Phil's life had been instrumental in him coming to faith. The first was the death of his grandfather which caused him to think deeply about death and the afterlife. The second was the birth of his first child. When his first baby was born he made contact with the local church to see about having the baby 'done'. The local vicar explained that there is much more significance to involvement with the Church than the christening of this little child, and took the opportunity to introduce Phil and his wife to the reality and dynamic of Christian faith. Through the service for their little baby, they were introduced to a personal and powerful Christian faith that was focused and centred on Jesus Christ.

There is a particular aspect to Phil's story that is very important. It speaks powerfully into the debate over what is often called 'prosperity theology'. There are some who say that if we give our lives to God, then God will bless and prosper us, and bring us success in our worldly life and career. It might seem to some that God has not particularly blessed Phil's professional career. As I mentioned in Chapter 4, his promising start under Brian Clough at Nottingham Forest has been followed by a series of moves to clubs that would be considered by the majority of people to be 'less glamorous'. The cynic might look at Phil's life, and ask the question, 'Well, what has God done for you in football?' But this is an important element of Phil Starbuck's story. God doesn't ask us to be successful, or, indeed, promise us success. The deal, if you like, is simply that we be faithful to God who calls us to serve him. He *may* bring us what the world would call success, or he may not bless us in that way. Our task is to be faithful to God and to walk humbly with him through life, and Phil's desire for that is clear and transparent. His Christian commitment, his zeal for God and his kingdom are there for all to see. It hasn't always been easy, and Phil has had his fair share of disappointment and frustration. Yet, in all of that, his faith in Jesus Christ has remained strong, firm, true and sure. The story of Phil Starbuck says that to be a follower of Jesus doesn't guarantee us success from a worldly point of view, but followers of Jesus are asked to be faithful and to continue making God and his ways their priority. That is what Phil has sought in life, and it's a great lesson for us who look on. I hope these stories from the world of football will help many to have a greater understanding of how God works in people's lives, and perhaps how they themselves can begin to find the reality of Christian faith. But there is perhaps one more thing that needs to be said.

There is always a danger when we stand a significant person – whether it be a sports personality, a prominent politician or a well-known entertainer – on a pedestal as a means of emphasising the Christian message. What I mean is this: the message is significant because of the content of the message. Just because people like Jonathan Edwards, Kriss Akabusi or Bernhard Langer stand up as Christians does not change the content of the message. The message is important as a message. It is perhaps helpful for well-known people to say, 'Yes, I believe it and it is true', but their affirming it doesn't make it true. I would want you to judge the message not because Alan West, Gavin Peacock, Dennis Bailey, Cyrille Regis or Phil Starbuck believe it, but because it is God's message.

It is important to emphasise this because there have been some people, prominent sportsmen among them, whose understanding of Christian faith has become changed from authentic Christian truth. I would defend their right to believe what they wish to believe, and even to express those beliefs in the media. However, there is much cause for concern when beliefs that are transparently not Christian are interpreted by some sections of the press and media as being standard Christian doctrine. The people whose stories I have told would affirm the truth of the basic Christian message. They would not lead you astray from authentic Christianity with references to a vague spirituality or some eclectic mix of acceptable religious ideas from a range of different sources. I believe they would stand for authentic Christian truth, but I say again that truth is truth whether these people affirm it or not. Jesus said, 'I am the Way, the Truth and the Life and no one comes to the Father except through Me.'

This chapter is called 'Memorable Meetings', in part because meeting with these individuals has been important for me. But the really memorable meeting, in each case, was the meeting these individuals had with the Saviour of the world, whose truth, love, power and forgiveness has changed their whole lives. If it's happened for them and it's happened for me, I'm sure it can happen for you, too.

9

The Referee – the Final Authority?

The question of authority, of rules and regulations, has long been considered by philosophers. I remember many animated discussions on the subject during my days as a theological student. However, it has probably never been debated so emotionally as of late in the world of football. The referee is given ultimate authority, but it seems to me, as an interested observer of the game, that the referee's job has got harder and harder over the years.

Before football was shown regularly on live TV I think the referee's job was relatively straightforward. He made his decisions as he saw them; players and spectators would agree or disagree, but the game proceeded and, for the most part, there was no documentary evidence to prove one way or the other. Once television was introduced, and particularly that wonderful device, the 'action replay', then key decisions and incidents could be put under review. Action replay really did revolutionise TV viewing. I remember hearing of a lady who, soon after its introduction, was watching a Cup Final with her husband. When a goal was scored and the action replay was shown, the lady remarked, 'Has the same man scored another one?' However, I think it is the advent of Sky's most excellent television coverage that has put even greater pressure on the referee. Suddenly it is not simply one or two camera angles, but sixteen or twenty camera angles focusing on the game. Our replay technology is very sophisticated. We can now not only see the action from a variety of camera angles, but also from a linesman's perspective or a referee's perspective and 'freeze frame' a particular sequence to see why at a particular moment in time an official may have made a particular decision. We may fail to appreciate that the referee, working his diagonal across the pitch and running hard to keep up with the play, does not have the capacity to freeze frame action as we have on TV. The referee makes his judgment as he sees it, and cannot be expected to get every decision right. We are back to the idea of perfection again. We've already considered the idea that no player is one hundred per cent perfect all of the time and described this fact as a parable of the state of humanity. In the same way, we shouldn't expect referees to be one hundred per cent right all of the time either.

As I talk to coaches and players I find their complaints are not directed to the small and difficult decisions that referees might get wrong from time to time. Their recurring concern is consistency. A goalkeeper rushing out of his area brings down an attacker and is 'red-carded'; the next week, in a similar scenario, a goalkeeper rushing out of the area and bringing down an attacker is 'yellow-carded'. There has to be consistency. No one wants to see the man sent off, but if the rule is the rule it should be applied. If it was operative last week, it should be operative this week. The rules needs to be applied on a consistent basis. Life in society demands rules and regulations, and these have to be followed for the good of all. In Britain it is the rule that everyone must drive on the left-hand side of the road. That rule, some may say, is restrictive. Maybe some of our European visitors would like to drive on the right. However, if others had the freedom to drive on the right, that would severely affect my freedom to drive on the left. The presence of rules is sometimes an aid to freedom.

Rules are essential in life, and rules are essential in sport. Why should we, therefore, expect spiritual matters to be any different? Why is it not reasonable for God to have set down certain rules and regulations about life and eternity?

The whole area of rules and authority is a big challenge to society today. We live in a 'pick and mix' society where individuals choose what they feel is right for them. The sense of 'absolute right' and 'absolute wrong' is increasingly being overtaken by a personal and individual morality. The comment is often made: 'Well, if that's OK for you, you do it.' 'If you think that's right for you, you follow it.' The individual's response to his or her circumstances becomes, in certain cases, the arbiter of whether a situation is right or wrong. If we accept that in a football game we need a referee to enforce what's right and what's wrong, even though he may be imperfect in his evaluations and judgments, is it not reasonable to accept God's verdict on right and wrong, if we accept his absolute goodness, righteousness, truthfulness and purity? If God is totally good, then his judgments are totally right. If his judgments are totally right, we need to accept what he says. If God speaks through the Scriptures about the sinfulness of humankind, and our need for forgiveness, then we need to take that on board.

I have sometimes used the traditional colours of Manchester United to convey in a simple way the essential message of the Christian gospel. Red, black and white are the colours found on the modern Manchester United first-choice shirts, their scarves, rosettes, and the vast variety of mementos that can be bought from the Megastore. I explain how the black reminds me of the dark side of our lives, and I quote the verse in Scripture that tells us that 'all have sinned and fall short of the glory of God' (Romans 3:23). The red reminds me of blood, and for Christians the blood of Jesus, shed on the cross at Calvary where Christ was crucified is of absolutely vital importance. We remember that death as we share bread and wine around the Communion table. In Colossians 1:19–20 we are told that God was in Christ and through Christ reconciled all things to himself by making peace through his blood shed on the cross. The third, traditional Manchester United colour, white, speaks to me of purity and holiness. Reading on from the verses just quoted, Paul says that Christians are reconciled by Christ's body through death to be presented holy in God's sight, without blemish and free from accusation, as long as they continue in the faith, and don't move from the hope that is found in the gospel (vv. 22–3). The Christian message is that the love and goodness of God, the favour that we don't deserve, can cover all that is wrong within our lives. God looks on us, not as dirty, stained, impure people, but as those who are without blemish and free from accusation. He sees us as pure and holy because of Christ's sacrifice on the cross.

That little outline story of the colours of Manchester

United begins with the idea that humankind is sinful. That idea doesn't originate simply in philosophy or in sociology, but has its root in the Christian Scriptures. The sinfulness, the moral and ethical poverty of humankind, the tainted nature of our beings and personalities, is a concept that is clearly taught in Scripture. It forces us to consider the question of whether we are willing to accept God's authority, his judgments, on our lives. Is there a parallel here with the referee in a game of football? The attacker shoots for a goal and the defender closes him down: there is a clash of bodies, the referee gives a corner kick. The defender says the ball came off the attacker last and it should be a goal kick. The attacker says that, before he even got near to the ball, the defender caught him first and it should be a penalty. They can express their opinions and argue their case, but if the referee gives a corner kick, then it is a corner kick, because the referee is the one with the authority. Each player may actually disagree with the referee's opinion, but because he is the referee that is the decision that counts. If a player fails to accept that decision he will face even more trouble. Can you imagine the defender walking up to the corner flag, picking up the ball, placing it on the goal line and taking a goal kick? He would be booked for that. Equally, if the attacker took the ball, placed it on the penalty spot and proceeded to take a penalty kick, he too could face a booking. Each would suffer the consequences of ignoring the referee's authority. Because he is the referee he has to be listened to. His judgment has to be accepted.

As human beings we may not like the idea of being described by the Scriptures as sinful. Again in Paul's letter to the Colossians, the apostle speaks of the characteristics of our earthly sinful nature: sexual immorality, impurity, lust, evil desires and greed. He also condemns anger, rage, malice, slander, filthy language, untruthfulness, and speaks quite bluntly about what is right and what is wrong. If we believe that Scripture has authority, and if we believe that God's view of life and lifestyle is not simply one opinion among many, then those words are very challenging to us. The Christian message seems to say that there are rights and wrongs. Morality is black and white; it is not simply shades of grey. The Scriptures seem to say that sin is a condition that affects us all, and the symptoms are expressed in individual actions or traits that God finds morally displeasing and spiritually damaging to us and to others. Such would seem to be God's evaluation of the condition of the human race. We can argue with God's assessment – we can tell the referee that the corner kick should be a goal kick, or the corner kick should be a penalty – but the authority figure makes his decision. If we accept the truth of the gospel, the authority of the Scriptures and the teaching of the Church, then we have to accept the challenge to our lives that comes through God's authoritative judgment on our situation.

Occasionally, managers, players and commentators applaud the referee: 'He's had a really good game.' 'His decisions were fine.' 'He helped the game flow and hang together.' 'He used his authority well.' I want to tell you that God's authority is always, ultimately, good. If we accept that authority and acknowledge that his message speaks to us of the morally broken and spiritually damaged nature of humanity's con-dition, then we can also accept God's answers and God's ways forward. God is not simply looking down on us to expose our weaknesses and to glory in the poverty of our condition. He shines the spotlight on our needs, and also points to a way forward, a way of hope and a way into the future. While the Scriptures challenge us about our moral and spiritual poverty they also point a way forward. They tell us that there is an answer to that condition. They tell us that the answer is in Jesus Christ. When we come under his authority we can find freedom. Under allegiance to him we find liberty. When we acknowledge our sinfulness through him, we can find forgiveness. God has the authority both to pinpoint and spotlight our sinfulness and the authority to declare that, through Christ, we are forgiven.

10

The Final Whistle

It is 5.00 a.m. on Wednesday 26 May, 1999. I am downstairs in our kitchen sitting at the breakfast table enjoying my normal porridge, toast and a mug of coffee, pondering the day that is before me. It is the day of the European Cup Final, and soon I must be meeting up with other members of staff and associates of MUFC at Manchester Airport to travel to Barcelona. Within an hour I am travelling through the back lanes of south-west Manchester from Sale through Timperley to Manchester Airport. In the departure lounge a throng of excited people contrast with the quiet, misty morning of the North Cheshire lanes. Man U are taking their staff to Barcelona for the European Cup Final.

Four days previously I had seen many of these faces on the staff trip to Wembley, and there had been great anticipation at the prospect of a 'Double', but the significance of the success against Newcastle United seemed to have been overshadowed by the possibilities that Barcelona was to bring. At Wembley, where Anne and I had sat amongst a whole crowd of Manchester United staff to enjoy that 2–0 victory, I had pondered much about the achievements of Sir Alex Ferguson, his staff and players. This was the third 'Double' of the 1990s. It was an awesome achievement, but once the Cup had been lifted the focus of all turned to the European Champions League Final. It would surely be an awesome spectacle.

It seemed to me that the club was taking every one of its employees and their associates to see the match in the Nou Camp. I mingled with the various groups of staff scattered throughout the concourse of the departure lounge. Despite the early hour the atmosphere was full of jollity, excitement and anticipation. Everyone seemed to be in good humour. I cannot remember how many times people said to me, 'Hello, Rev., I hope you've prayed hard today.' I gave the same reply to each and every enquiry, to the effect that, yes I had, but not for a result: I am the chaplain – not a witch doctor. I find that people are innately superstitious. They seem to see the chaplain as someone who is there to confer God's blessing on proceedings, and in some way persuade God that the result should go our way rather than the opposition's.

I was once at a Baptist minister's gathering where three or four of us were involved in a discussion about football club chaplaincy. One of the ministers posed the question, 'Do you actually pray for them to win then? Do you pray for good results at Old Trafford?' Before I had a chance to answer another one piped up 'Don't be silly, the chaplain doesn't have to do that at Old Trafford. With the manager and team they've got, you don't have to pray for victory. They can achieve it without God's intervention.' I said then, as I said at the airport, that chaplains aren't witch doctors.

Although most of the comments people make about a chaplain's possible influence on results are simply superficial silly banter, it is vitally important that I, and other chaplains, really knock this issue on the head. The results of a football team are the responsibility of the manager, coaches and players. We cannot even follow the tendency which I thought I detected in one manager who, when the team won, would say, 'We've done well today', but when they lost, would express the opinion that 'They didn't play at all today'. Whether the team wins or whether the team loses, the chaplain has no major part to play. His role is to provide the pastoral and spiritual safety net, not to be the lucky mascot. Unfortunately, people do tend to see you as at least having the potential to bestow the goodness and the grace of God on normal, everyday proceedings.

Having collected my ticket and sorted out the boarding pass, I made my way to the particular chartered jumbo jet that I had been allocated to. Considering the number of planes chartered by Manchester United Football Club, the air corridors into Barcelona must have been particularly busy that day. At 8.00 a.m. we taxied along the runway to wait for our take-off slot, but some two-thirds along the runway we pulled in to a side parking bay. There were technical problems. I heard the pilot reporting that there seemed to be some trouble with the number three engine. There was then a clear announcement to the entire plane that technical staff were being called in to examine a problem. Not long after a ladder appeared, taking an engineer onto the starboard wing where he began to take away engine cowlings and examine the inner working's of the two starboard engines. While this was happening someone in the seats behind tapped me on the shoulder and pointed out that, in view of all that was going on, they found it really comforting that the club chaplain was on the plane. I remember thinking that, in view of the fact that the club chaplain was on the plane, I didn't find what was going on terribly comforting. But that was purely a personal and selfish view. A few others joined in and said, 'You'd better pray for us, Rev.' Eventually, the engineers seemed to give the pilot the go-ahead and we were able to resume the slow trundle down to the runway and our flight to Barcelona.

We were met at the airport and taken to a wonderful hotel near the marina where we had a lovely lunch in the warm Catalonian spring sunshine. A wonderful variety of seafood with bread and wine was arrayed on our tables, and then much later on we were given a main course of either steak or fish. There was a chance to walk around the marina area before the coaches that had brought us there took us on to the Nou Camp Stadium, which we reached maybe a couple of hours before kick-off time. The atmosphere was already electric. We then walked the half-mile from the bus parking area to the magnificent Nou Camp Stadium. Outside, North-western accents were strongly in the air and the red, black and white of Manchester United seemed to be everywhere. I took a few photographs, but decided, with such a huge crowd around and about the stadium, it would be wise to get in early. I passed through an outer security check and then to the inner turnstiles and made my way up to a bank of seats in the middle tier overlooking the goalmouth. The stadium looked magnificent and was filling slowly in the evening sunshine. I remember the cheers, shouts and applause as our own players came out to sample the atmosphere and to look at the stadium before the game, and I remember the boos and the catcalls as the Munich players did the same, parading before their fans at the far end of the stadium. The atmosphere was building steadily, and the empty seats around me were gradually filling with people swathed in red, black and white. As the pre-match entertainment began, I became engaged in conversation with those around me.

The seat on my left had been allocated to Norman Davies, who had been the kit man at Manchester United for many years and had retired three years earlier. His deputy, Albert, had taken over the job which is a remarkably onerous responsibility. The fact that Norman was there spoke volumes to me about the generosity of MUFC and their concern for detail. Norman was no longer an employee of the club, but, on this occasion, in view of his past involvement, the invitation was there for him to be present. To my right was Doc McHugh, another former associate of the club. Doc McHugh was the official club doctor when I arrived in 1992 and had been involved with the club for years before then. He had retired three years earlier and Dr Michael Stone had taken over his role. Dr Stone had become a full-time doctor with the club and travelled with the first team squad wherever they went. He was already in Barcelona with the club party, but again I was thrilled to see Doc McHugh there. Next to him was Mr Jonathan Noble, the club orthopaedic surgeon. 'Hello, Reverend,' he said when he saw me. 'How good to see you here. By the way, how's your medial meniscus cartilage?' I'd seen Mr Noble at his National Health clinic in the May of 1998, having needed some knee surgery. However, the pre-surgery check, which is standard in Trafford for all hospital patients over forty five, did not go as expected. The ECG test had revealed questions about heart function, and I had my cartilage surgery postponed until the cardiology department of the hospital had done a thorough investigation to check out any potential problems. Thankfully, more ECGs and eventually an angiogram revealed that the heart was still in good nick. This is what I had suspected, and I was now on the orthopaedic waiting list again. In the midst of the pre-match excitement at the Nou Camp Stadium I found myself talking with Jonathan Noble about the conclusions of the cardiac investigations and my hopes that the hospital would now go ahead with the elective surgery on my knee.

Conversations ceased as the teams came out, anthems were played and kick-off was awaited. Norman Davies and I spoke at length at half-time. Our assessment was that the team hadn't played terribly well and we probably didn't deserve much more than to be 1–0 down from that early free kick. We expressed our sadness again that Club Captain, Roy Keane, and Paul Scholes were missing, and we looked at various options for the second half. What a great game football is because, while those that really know about the game are making their right and appropriate judgments, we who are simply spectators with an amateur interest and very limited understanding can none the less express our opinions too. We awaited the second half with hope and with interest. However, that hope didn't seem terribly justified. With a wonderfully flowing move the Germans hit Schmeichel's right-hand post and the ball bounced back into his hands. Norman nudged me, 'It could have been two, Rev.! We could be two down.' 'We're not, Norman, we're not,' I said. A little while later they hit the woodwork again, an overhead kick crashing against the bar, rebounding to one of our players in a crowded penalty box, and it was hit clear. Norman grabbed me again, 'Could be a good sign that, Rev., could be a really good sign. Perhaps things will go for us.'

'Perhaps,' I replied. 'Perhaps it is Norman, but equally it could be a terrible sign: we could be three down. Perhaps it says we're not getting to grips with their attack at all.'

'Maybe,' said Norman, 'but perhaps it says they're not going to score any more goals. As long as we're 1–0 down we're in with a chance.'

I believed that was true. As the minutes ticked by, there were substitutions and changes and some signs of hope, but no goals were forthcoming.

The clock at the far end had begun to show eighty minutes plus, and the crowd around me oscillated between more and more vocal urgings and a sense that perhaps it just wasn't to be our day. As the clock moved from eighty-nine to ninety I remembered thinking that that was probably it. I recalled a quote from Gary Lineker who once said: 'Football is a simple game: you pass and tackle, battle and shoot, but it goes into extra time and the Germans win on penalties', or something to that effect. As we entered the ninety-first minute I remember thinking it would be a bonus even if we got to extra time, but I consoled myself with the thought that really it hadn't been a bad day. We had got here safely; we had had a wonderful lunch; I had enjoyed a lot of good conversations with many, many people; I was sitting in a stadium in Barcelona watching a European Cup Final, and at least United had got there. Such were my private musings; I certainly didn't plead with God Almighty to intervene in a wondrous way, and I didn't bargain with God that, if he would give us a victory, I would do this or that or the other. As a United attack down our left flank was repulsed for a corner and David Beckham went over to take the kick, I do remember talking to the Lord. I didn't ask for a goal and I didn't ask for a victory, but I remember saying, almost with an attitude of resignation, 'Well, Lord, if it's part of your purposes that we win this trophy, then we really do need your intervention very soon.' The Good Lord knows me well enough that I would never now ask for the power and purposes of God to be focused on the result of a football match. By saying what I did say to the Lord then I felt I was focusing, not on the result, but on the purposes of God. I wasn't even affirming that this would be part of the purposes of God, but was simply raising the question. There was then some theological depth and perhaps some Christian maturity in what I was saying at that moment in time. I wasn't seeking to blackmail God, and I wasn't asking him for something that was only a selfish request. Mind you, at that very moment in time there could have been many thousands of prayers being uttered – basic English prayers like 'God, help us score,' or maybe basic German prayers like 'God, keep them out.' Who is to tell?

I watched, more in hope than belief, as David Beckham knocked in that corner. At the far post it was half-cleared and fell to Ryan Giggs near the edge of the penalty box. From around the edge of the D he half-hit a shot towards the goal, which was intercepted by Teddy Sheringham. He swung a leg and again didn't connect properly, but there was sufficient contact to scuff the ball into the bottom corner of the net. We were on our feet as soon as the corner kick had come in and we had seen the movement of the goal net in front of us. The sight of the ball nestling behind the German goalkeeper, hand still raised appealing for off-side, sent the United fans wild. I found myself jumping up and down with Norman Davies, as he clung on to me and I to him in order to maintain a degree of balance as we pogoed ecstatically. Even Doc McHugh and Jonathan Noble, the body side of what was obviously a body and soul grouping of this row of the stand, were on their feet with hands raised in the air. Norman shouted at me above the hubbub. 'We'll win it, we'll win it now, we'll win it in extra time. The Germans'll never recover from that.' The contrast between the United end and the Bayern end was marked. We were still celebrating the equaliser when another attacking foray led to yet another corner. The crowd were singing, shouting and cheering as David Beckham took the kick again. All I remember was a near-post header and a far-post lunge from Ole Gunnar Solksjaer, and the ball nestled in the back of the net. For half a moment I needed to be sure that we had scored. Had Ole Gunnar's shot gone in or hit the side netting? I felt I could see the ball behind the despairing German defenders on the line, safe and secure within the net. I certainly saw the apparent scorer sprinting and then sliding on his knees towards the byline as he celebrated what would surely be a match-winning goal. The facts were confirmed with the sight of the Bayern defenders distraught, scattered on the ground, and hundreds of United fans in ecstatic unbelief, jumping, dancing, singing, shouting, hugging anything that was near. In the third minute of injury time United had snatched the game 2–1. It was like a dream, a storyline from some *Roy of the Rovers* magazine, or a 'footie soap' on TV. If this had happened in the world of fiction it would be too far-fetched to be believed, but it had happened in front of our very eyes. With incredible character and determination, way into the depths of injury time the European Cup had been won.

The bouncing throng around was still enraptured. A whole cluster of United players had mobbed Solksjaer and celebrated with him in front of the United end. Others on the bench had run across to add their congratulations and the United squad was now regrouping for kick-off. The referee was making his way to the German penalty box where he had physically to encourage some of the players to stand up and get on with the game. They were distraught and utterly devastated. With ninety minutes on the clock they were entering time added on 1–0 up and apparently coasting to victory in the Champions Cup. Three minutes later they were to be deemed losers, and some obviously did not even want to bother playing the final twenty seconds of the match. The unbelievable had happened and all too quickly.

I was told it happened far too quickly for Lennart Johansson, the President of UEFA. As the clock moved from eighty-nine to ninety minutes he left his seat in the VIP area, put a sympathetic hand on Sir Bobby Charlton's shoulder and made his way down to take part in the presentation of the Cup to the Bayern Munich team. He descended a flight of internal stairs and came towards the area leading onto the pitch where the presentation would be made at the end of the proceedings. He was told by an official that United had equalised and he had better return to his seat and wait the outcome of extra time. So, he turned round and made the journey all the way up the stairs again to resume his position in the VIP seating area. However, as he was about to enter the VIP box again, the steward at the top of the stairway explained to him that a winning goal had been scored by Manchester United and Mr Johansson would be needed downstairs in a short while to make the presentation. He turned round again to trek down to the pitch side once more. The final whistle had gone, and several minutes later he was involved in presenting the European Cup to Manchester United, having seen neither of the goals that they had scored to win it. That night was memorable and the climax was utterly unforgettable, but let me draw a couple of spiritual parables from that situation.

There is an old saying that it's not over until the fat lady sings, and the Munich team, although winning as the game entered injury time, had not won, because the final whistle had not blown. The winners are not those who are winning when the clock shows ninety minutes, but those who are winning when the referee blows the final whistle. Life is like a football match in the sense that we have an idea or a hope of how long it might last, but we are never sure when the final whistle will be blown. The hope used to be that we would attain to three score years and ten, but now that is regarded as a young age to depart this life. Can we hope for eighty, eighty-five or ninety or more? The truth is that we do not know when life's final whistle will be blown, but we do know that it will come. Along with taxation it is the only certainty in life. What Jesus Christ offers us is the assurance that when that whistle goes we can be certain that we are on the winning side.

At the Nou Camp on the 26 May 1999 the despair and devastation of the losers was plain for all to see. Some sat dazed, some beat the ground with their fists, some were lying prostrate on the floor unable to move. The whistle had blown and they were the losers. The amazing truth of the Christian message is that it is possible for us to know that when life's final whistle comes we will not be losers, but winners. We can know before injury time, before the ninety minutes are up. If we respond early enough, we can even know before half-time that we will be on God's winning side.

But the challenge is, whose side are we on? If that final whistle were to blow today, would you go on to take the trophy and God's winners' medal? The Christian gospel says that it is possible to know, even before the whistle goes, whether we are winners or losers. We are told in what is probably the most famous verse in the Bible that 'God so loved the world that he gave his one and only Son that whoever believes in him shall not perish, but shall have eternal life.' We are told that there is now no condemnation for those who are 'in Christ Jesus'. Through these and many other Scriptures we are assured that the individual who has come to taste the goodness and forgiveness of God will know God with them through life and into eternity. When we become a Christian, God's Spirit comes to live and stay with us so that even when the body dies, the Spirit of Christ Jesus living within our spiritual dimension causes us to live eternally because God's Spirit is eternal. There is a greater ultimate hope of a new heaven and a new earth, of our spirit being clothed with a new resurrection body. The Christian view of the future is of an ultimate and absolute and final redemption. Salvation is past and present and future. The Christian knows that they have been saved; they know they are being saved as God works in them; and they know ultimately the extent and totality of that salvation will be theirs. Life, as we know it, will confront us with a final whistle, but for the Christian that is the doorway through to the presentation ceremony and a celebration party that will last forever. The Gospel of Jesus Christ invites us now to consider which side we would like to be on – the winning side or the losing side.

I heard a story about what the Manchester United manager said to the players at half-time in Barcelona. Normally, I would not choose to use this for fear of being accused of name dropping, or being misunderstood in some other way, but the story has an awesome parallel, and is just too good for me to waste. Sir Alex had been talking to Steve Archibald, the former Spurs favourite who had played in a European Final against Barcelona, but his team had been defeated. For Steve, the greatest pain was not when the final whistle blew, but when the medals and trophies were being presented at the end. As the team assembled at the presentation rostrum to receive their losers' medals, they saw the trophy that could have been theirs. Yet, because they were losers, they were not able to touch it. They could see it, and they could imagine what might have been, but they could not lay a hand on it, because that joy and privilege belonged to the winners. At half-time in Barcelona, Sir Alex told the team this story to provide them with both challenge and inspiration to take out with them into the second half. The question is: do you just want to look at the trophy, or do you want to get hold of it and make it your very own?

This is another parable with a very powerful challenge, because the Christian faith presents us with the same alternative. Do we want to look at the trophy, or do we want to get hold of it and make it our very own? Many people just want to look at the idea of believing in Jesus Christ and following him. Some are strong enough to look at the idea, and say, 'That is what I need. That is what will deal with the emptiness in my life, that is what will deal with the dirt, the shame, the failure and the frustration.' Those people do all that they can to reach out and get hold of it. It is helpful to think about spiritual things and all that is involved in Christian faith, but thinking about it isn't sufficient. The challenge is to get hold of it, and to make it ours in such a way that we know we have won the trophy that is above all other trophies, the trophy that lasts for eternity.

11

The Biggest Match of All

Perhaps nothing can top the drama and excitement of the 1999 European Cup Final for Manchester United fans and, I hope, for other followers of English football. For all who were there the images and memories of that evening, and the days following, will never be forgotten.

I obviously remember the tumultuous reception given to the United players by their fans, but I also appreciate the hugely generous applause and acknowledgment from the Bayern fans at the opposite end of the stadium. It did make me wonder whether, if the boot had been on the other foot and United had been winning only to lose in extra time, our own fans would have been as gracious and as generous to the German team. I'll always remember how the Man United squad gathered at the United end of the ground, with each player coming up to hold the Cup and to conduct the crowd in his individual celebration routine.

I remember landing in Manchester Airport at about 5.00

a.m., taking two or three members of staff back to their various homes, and then eventually getting back to my house in Sale at about 5.45 a.m. The first thing I did was to make a cup of tea, and sit in front of the television and rerun the video of the last ten minutes of the game, just to check what exactly happened in those awesome minutes of extra time. I also remember going with the family to a junction on the A56 when the team eventually returned from Barcelona and began their awesome victory parade into the centre of Manchester. We parked the car and joined the crowd of thousands that had lined the route into the city centre to watch the open-top bus with the trophies gleaming and the team waving and smiling. They were receiving the deserved adulation of their fans.

Was it the greatest football match of the season or of the decade? Perhaps that depends on whom you support, or whether you look for skill, excitement and goals, or tactics as teams try to work against each other. Or, do you look at the occasion and the importance of a result in order to make your judgment as to what is a great match or not? Do you consider character, and, if you do, how does the character needed to pull a team up from being 1–0 down in injury time compare with that awesome Cup semi-final against Arsenal in the same season when they were a man down in extra time? As I said before, the wonderful thing about football is that it is a game of opinions, and we would all express our opinion about the match of the last decade, or even the match of any particular season.

Throughout this book we have found in football a rich source of wisdom and truth which has much to teach us in our spiritual lives. I now want to bring these together and draw up my top spiritual 'coaching tips', or advice, for getting into God's team.

Number one: Understand the basics

In 1979 I was asked to attend an international sports ministry conference in Washington, DC. While I was there I met the man who was the chaplain to the Washington Redskins American Football Team. He was interested in my work at Watford Football Club, and we exchanged notes on our respective work. On the Sunday he invited me to the morning chapel service that was put on for the Washington Redskins at their overnight hotel, and then, after a bite of lunch, we went on to see the game.

It was my first ever experience of American Football, and I found it very hard to understand. The game didn't seem to flow; it was constantly being interrupted, and, whenever it was, there was a great hubbub with loads of players seeming to invade the pitch and mingling all over the place. Eventually, the pitch was cleared of some of them and they would get on with the game. Also, in the middle of the game people would get up and walk out to buy popcorn or drinks, and then return later, but they did all this while the game was going on. It was distinctly different from anything I had been used to. As the afternoon progressed I began to find out more about the game as I asked questions like: how much longer is there? Are games always so disjointed? I came to find out that there was actually an attacking team and a defending team. It really helped me when I grasped that the game was broken up into little sections of offence of defence – one of the basic concepts of the game, really, but I hadn't understood it and no one had explained it to me. After that, the game became clearer to me.

I believe the Church today must develop a capacity for explaining some of the basic concepts of the faith to those who want to find out what we really are saying. Our starting point must not be with the particular details, but with the broad and simple ideas.

Number two: Consider the coaching manual

If we are to learn more than just the simple basics of a game, then we need to find a source that will provide more detailed information. When I was involved in managing and coaching Torino, in the Grimsby Saturday League Division Four, I, and one or two others, realised we needed some help if we were to get the team to lose less often, to concede fewer goals and to score more than we were doing. So we bought two or three coaching books. Today, our first choice might not be Alan Hardacre's *Football for Schoolboys*, but, whatever books or videos we pick up, it makes sense for those who are wanting to have a better understanding of football and a greater knowledge of how to play the game more effectively, to find some help.

It is always good advice to read the instructions early on. Have you ever bought flat-pack furniture and decided to put it together without reference to the instructions? After two hours of hassle and aggravation we realise the wisdom of following the maker's instructions. It's the same in life, it's the same in sport, and it's the same spiritually. There is great wisdom in reading the manual, and not as a last resort. We should be encouraging people to read our spiritual manual early on, but they may need help in doing so. If we give them the Old and New Testaments in a closely printed, tiny Bible, in the language of a bygone era, they may experience great difficulty in understanding it. After all, it is quite reasonable to begin a book at the front and work towards the end, but that may not always prove the most effective way for someone starting out to read the Bible and seeking to understand the Christian faith more fully. There are books and booklets which might present one of the Gospels in an attractive and interesting way with pictures, explanations, maps, testimonies, teaching and preaching points scattered throughout. Let us try to give those who are developing a little spiritual appetite, small bite-size pieces of Scripture that will be helpful and digestible. Why not start with a Gospel?

Number three: Talk with those who play the game

One of the ways that we can learn a lot about a particular sport is not simply by reading a manual or watching a coaching video, but by actually talking to those who play it, preferably those who have got a little further than we have and who are doing reasonably well. We can ask how they got started, how they began to improve, and what areas are important to sort out at an early stage. I remember when I was being taught tennis as a schoolboy. I found my game improved enormously once I had understood the correct way to grip the racket for various shots. Our teacher could see that I was having a problem and helped me immediately to overcome it.

One of the exciting things that I see at Manchester United Football Club is some of the older professionals, or some of the youth coaches, helping the younger players individually. The coach may say, 'I was watching you on Saturday morning, and I saw you did that. Why did you do that? If you're faced with that situation again, here are two things that you could do that might work better, and this one is the best of all.' Experience is passed on.

The same applies spiritually. If people are interested in discovering more about the truth of the Christian message and how it impacts the lives of people today, then they will find it really helpful to ask questions of people who are already Christians, whose lives have been changed, and who have found the reality and power of that message themselves.

Number four: Talk with the manager

In a football team the manager knows what he wants from a particular group of players; he understands why they are being put together to form a team. He knows the particular tasks he wants each player to perform. A team talk before a match, therefore, becomes quite significant because the manager explains how he wants the team to play on this particular occasion. It is very important for players to hear from the manager. The same is true spiritually. We need to have a sense of what Jesus Christ wants from us, and we need to develop our prayer life so that we can speak honestly and openly with God. Bible reading and prayer are excellent devotional practices to develop. They will help us build our relationship with the One who wants to be our Lord and Saviour.

It is important to begin to pray, and I know many people who have begun to pray even before they have made a Christian commitment. Many may have initially said to God, 'Lord, I'm not sure if you're there, but I really need you to reveal yourself to me if you are there.' That little prayer has been the beginning of a huge spiritual revolution.

Number five: Keep trying

Football history is full of stories of players who were not supremely talented, but kept trying to make the most of the talent that they had. They were the sort of players who worked hard at their fitness and kept practising their skills; they endeavoured to make the most of the talent they had, and some of them did more than make a reasonable living from the world of football.

There is a message here for those who want to come to a real understanding of who God is and how he can break into the lives of ordinary people today. The teaching of Jesus about seeking and knocking is very important. He said, 'Seek and you will find; knock and the door will be opened to you.' There are some people who are not really serious about their questions about God. Their questions are reasons and excuses for not believing. Those sorts of questions are a defence mechanism against considering Christian faith more profoundly or more seriously. However, there are some people whose questions are genuine; they ask because they want to find real answers. They knock on the door because they want to find an opening and a way forward. It is often helpful to find out what sort of person we're dealing with. Is it someone who genuinely wants to find God, or is it someone whose questioning is really a defence mechanism? We should encourage the genuine enquirers who are sincere and keep seeking. We need to do all that we can to help that seeking process.

Number six: Understand the opposition

Any player in a football game who wants to take his sport seriously will find great benefit in understanding the opposition. At the professional level this might involve a scout going on two or three missions to look at the pattern of play of the opposition, to try to focus on their potential weaknesses and strengths, and to bring a report back so that his own players may know what to expect. At a local amateur level it might mean trying to work out if the player who is against you is stronger on his left foot than his right. Is he quick and pacey, or is he firm but strong in the tackle? Is he good on the floor or in the air? If you can work out, in the first ten or fifteen minutes, the relative strengths and weaknesses of your opponent, it might help you a great deal in the match that you are playing.

Spiritually, we need to know about the opposition. We need to encourage people to realise that they are involved in a bit of a spiritual battle. It is not enough for them simply to come to an understanding about God, Jesus Christ and the work of the Holy Spirit. That is very important, but, as we said much earlier in this book, the Christian is involved in a transfer. There is a move from the kingdom of darkness into the kingdom of God's Son. Those who are thinking seriously about faith and who are seeking to know God are really in a spiritual tug-of-war.

They need to know the enemy and his strategy. They need to understand what temptation is all about, and how the Evil One may throw confusion and uncertainty across the path of those who are seeking God. We need to explain to those who actually commit themselves to become Christians, and are beginning to get involved in the life of their church, that they may be the focus of the Enemy's attacking strategies. We don't want to see the Devil behind every little disaster and broken fingernail, but we do need to be aware of, and understand, the teaching of passages like Ephesians 6, which introduces us to the reality of spiritual warfare, and explains how the Christian can stand against the attacks of the Evil One. The seeker, the young Christian, and indeed, the older, more mature Christian all need to be aware of how the Enemy will seek to tempt us away from the ways of God. To be aware of his opposition is very important and good advice.

Number seven: Join a team and find your position

Just as it is possible to play football outside the context of a team, practising skills on your own, sometimes kicking a ball against a wall, or joining in with two or three mates whenever that can be organised, it is much more satisfying to be a member of a team, and to develop your particular skills in an appropriate position. This is indispensable advice for those who are seeking to take the claims of Jesus seriously. We need to be able to help them bridge the gap between small group or individual situations and to become active and involved members of the Church.

This is quite challenging for many people. They enjoy a bit of chat and conversation with close friends who are Christians; they might even be happy with a small group discussion setting. But we need to take them beyond that, and help them appreciate that Christian faith is not an individual but a team sport. We need to help them become team players, and we need to help them find their position in that team.

Of course, they will thrive best in a successful team. We, therefore, need to help people find churches where there is spiritual life and spiritual food. We need to help people get involved in churches where there is a sense of God at work by his Spirit, where the people have a lively faith, and where that faith is being demonstrated in community involvement, in work, in witness and mission. The Scriptures also need to be taught and explained helpfully so that the congregation finds that there is spiritual food to nurture them. Yet, equally, we need to appreciate that the perfect church is difficult to find this side of glory. Christians may be redeemed sinners, but sometimes the old nature shows through. We must be realistic as we talk about life in the local church, but it is essential that we help our serious seeker or our young Christian to find the encouragement and support that they will need through joining the local church.

Number eight: Injuries

In the football club, whether it's at a professional or an amateur level, we will find that some of our players get injured. This might either occur in training or in matches. It could be a minor 'niggly' thing that lasts a short time, or a major thing that takes them out for longer. It may be important to explain to the potential follower of Jesus Christ that there are times when we may feel injured in his service.

We are complex creatures: we can suffer disappointment and can feel 'let down'. We can feel unsupported or isolated. We can feel that too much is expected of us. We can feel weary and overburdened by the responsibility that is given to us. We can feel drained by giving out more than we are taking in, or, alternatively, we can feel spiritually overweight and unfit because we are taking in and taking in, but not engaging in any spiritual exercise at all. We must encourage potential disciples of Jesus to do all that they can to keep spiritually fit and strong, and to be able to cope with the challenge and difficulty of spiritual injury when that comes along.

The church too needs to be taught how to care for its

injured saints. We are involved in spiritual warfare; we are soldiers of Christ, and sometimes soldiers in battle suffer injuries. There is a need at times to pull someone out of the front line to give them the care and support that will enable them to recuperate and become fit and strong again, so that they can go on to serve God again at a future time. Sadly, there are some churches who seem to be more inclined to shoot their injured than to help them through recuperation and rehabilitation.

Number nine: Representing your team well

In professional sport there is an increasing emphasis on the importance of representing the team. It extends well beyond the field of play. Players and associates are being made more and more aware of their public profile. Their involvement in professional sport may give them a very privileged position, but with it comes great responsibilities. We now see sports stars generally, and football players in particular, doing excellent work representing their club in the community, in hospitals and with the underprivileged and needy. A wide variety of causes benefit from this sort of commitment and involvement. Players and representatives will normally come along with club tracksuit or club blazer and tie, so clearly demonstrating that they represent their particular club.

Again, we can see a spiritual parallel. Those called into Jesus Christ's team, those who come under his management, are expected to represent him in the world outside the Church. Those who are considering the challenge of Christian faith need to understand that making Jesus Christ their Lord affects every area of their lives. It is a personal decision, but it's more than that. It involves our becoming an active member in a local community of Christians, but it's more than that, too. It involves not only serving God in the Church, but also serving him in the wider world. It involves showing the world by deed, by lifestyle, and sometimes by words, that we really do belong to Jesus Christ. In Colossians 3, a passage we have already considered, Paul challenges us to 'put to death', or get rid of, characteristics, attitudes, traits and behaviour that are part of our old nature and distinctly not Christian. He encourages us to put on, to 'clothe' ourselves with, new characteristics which become our new garments to be worn as the identifying clothes of God's chosen people.

The player, representing his club at a community function, might be wearing his club blazer and tie, or his club tracksuit. He is identifiable by what he wears. In the same way Christians should be identifiable, not by their normal clothing but by their character clothing. The characteristics of our godless, fallen, sinful nature have to go. Paul's list in Colossians 3:5–9 is very specific and precise. Characteristics like immorality, greed, anger, malice and lying are not congruent with Christian faith and lifestyle. Instead, Christians should be characterised by compassion, humility, patience and a for-giving spirit. As Christians we represent Jesus, our Lord, in the world not simply by wearing a jacket or a tie embroidered with a sign of the cross or the symbol of a fish. We represent Christ to the world by our character and by our lifestyle.

Thus, the challenge to those contemplating Christian commitment must include not simply an understanding of the basic Christian message and how to respond to it, but the fuller implications of Christian discipleship. The issue is not simply to say yes to Jesus at the end of an evangelistic event, or at the end of an Alpha course. The call of Christ is that we come and follow him, and part of that following is that we are seen to be 'Jesus people', not just on Sunday morning at 10.30 but every day of our lives. In other words, by what we are and by what we do, we represent Christ and his kingdom to the world.

However, we mustn't frighten new Christians with these implications; we need to assure them that God, by his Holy Spirit, will help us to be good representatives of Christ in the world. We need to encourage them by assuring them that other Christians will help them, strengthen them and support them, and that the prayers, fellowship and teaching of the Church will be behind them. They mustn't feel that they are alone in representing Jesus Christ and his disciples.

To summarise then: for all of us who are Christians there must be three overlapping areas of responsibility. The first is personal: my own sense of God's love for me, and my response to the gospel of Christ and his call to follow him. The second is corporate: it concerns my involvement with the community of God's people, which is the local Christian church. It is there that I need to be involved worshipping, witnessing and working for God amongst the fellowship of his people. The third is the circle of the wider world: it confronts us with the need to live out our Christian life in the world that is beyond our church walls, and outside the view through our church windows.

Number ten: Keep your enthusiasm

If there is one final spiritual coaching tip that we can glean from the world of football, it would be to encourage disciples of Jesus Christ to maintain their enthusiasm. Time and time again we see managers being interviewed on TV about one of their senior players. The player may now be into his thirties, he may have achieved a great deal in the past, and the manager is asked how important he is to the club. The manager explains that his influence is wonderful; his enthusiasm is as strong as it was when he was a teenager; he does his very best in training; he's always chirpy and buoyant; he tries to help the younger lads; he's willing to accept responsibilities; he always gives one hundred per cent; he's a tremendous example. A player with that sort of experience and enthusiasm is a priceless asset to any football club.

We need people in our churches who continue in their enthusiasm for God's kingdom, who maintain the zeal of early Christian devotion and the excitement of learning to live the 'Jesus way'. If football managers applaud the continuing vitality and zeal of some of their mature players, then how much more would our churches benefit from the continuing enthusiasm of their members. One church leader said to me that he felt the typical church congregation could be divided into three groups: a third of them were highly involved and enthusiastic; another third were very appreciative of those who were highly involved and enthusiastic, and supported and applauded them; the final third wondered why the middle third were clapping!

If Christians have found something as important and significant as they say they have, then surely we should maintain our enthusiasm and our zeal for that cause – for Christ and for the growth of his kingdom. This is far more important than the transient material pleasures and benefits that life has to offer. I don't think God is against wealth and riches in themselves, as long as they are used wisely and well in a way that honours him. Famous or wealthy Christians can use their influence or riches for the glory of God and the growth of his Kingdom. It is sad, though, when society so often feels that meaning in life and personal satisfaction and happiness are conditional on wealth, possessions, influence and power – things that we would broadly describe as 'material'. They may enable us to lead a more comfortable life, but they may not bring a more purposeful one, and they certainly won't introduce us to the personal peace and purpose that can be found through Jesus Christ.

Living for him is the best way to spend our lives. Knowing him and his love, serving him and his purposes, is not simply the way to find meaning and fullness in life here and now. It promises hope beyond the grave and into eternity. In life and in death the Christian knows that God's love, grace, mercy and commitment to us last into eternity, way beyond life's final whistle.

12

Post-match Comments

It is ten minutes to five on a Saturday, and for the management, staff and players at a football club the main event of the day is over. The game is finished, its final whistle has blown, and all have gathered back in the changing room. There is either the bubbly atmosphere of jubilation and congratulation or the deadly quietness of frustration and defeat. It is a time when the manager may have two important tasks to perform.

The first is to speak to his players generally, as a group, about the performance of that afternoon and to consider, whether win, lose or draw, the positives and the negatives that can be learnt from the afternoon's performance. His second task may be to confront the media. Whether local, national or international journalists or representatives of various TV companies, they all have their questions, and the manager must consider them and answer them wisely. In these two conversations, he draws together all the strands that have been involved in the ninety minutes of football, and, indeed, what has gone before it and what will flow from it.

In this chapter I want to do a sort of 'post-match team talk' and press conference. The tendency of preachers is to say what they are going to say, then to say it, and finally to summarise what they have said. This chapter is not intended to be a repetitive summary, but it does touch on some of the ideas that have appeared so far. I want to commend to you Christian faith, particularly if you do not currently subscribe to it. We live in a very secular world and many would scoff at the idea of belief in a God who is eternal, majestic, glorious, all-knowing, all-seeing, filled with love, grace and mercy, and who has a concern for people like us. Others, who might agree that such a God could exist, may scoff at the idea that it is possible for us to know that God in a personal way. Yet more may dispute that there is only one way to know him personally, and that pathway is the person of Jesus Christ. If these ideas are a problem to you I am sorry; they are not simply my ideas, but the concepts of traditional Christian teaching contained in the traditional Christian creeds and rooted in Scripture. Clearly, we acknowledge the significance of other faiths and the importance of other faith communities, but I am at pains to stress that there is something unique about the Christian claim. Central to the Christian faith is the person of Jesus Christ, his life, death and resurrection. Other religions may point to great teachers or great philosophers who left a wonderful inheritance in the form of teachings and sayings, holy writings and philosophies to those who would follow, but Christianity is distinctly different. It doesn't look back to a grave where the body of the founder is laid: Christianity is unique because it believes that its founder is God, that Jesus is God in human form – God incarnate. It believes that this is proved by his resurrection. Jesus Christ actually died, yet came to life again and ascended into heaven. God, the Holy Spirit, has come from heaven to work in the Church and in the lives of those who become followers of Jesus Christ.

This unique message requires careful consideration. The followers of Jesus Christ come from different backgrounds, and find faith in many different ways. Some may be from a religious background and may always have had a sense of the presence of God, yet, suddenly, the bits of the jigsaw come together: the light is turned on. They see how it all hangs together. The familiar suddenly takes on a new significance. That is the experience of many who have had a God-fearing church background. They suddenly come to a realisation of what the ritual, majesty, liturgy and activity of the Church really means.

There are many others who come to find this life-changing faith from a distinctly secular background. It may be the very poverty of that secularism that causes them to ponder the possibility of God and faith. Some come suddenly, many come slowly. For some it could be the personal experience of a majestic vista from a high mountain or the contemplation of the glory of the heavens observed on a cloudless night in the middle of the countryside away from all artificial lighting. For others it may be a visit to the fervour and vitality of a church service or a Christian meeting, or being part of a small group that is looking at Christian religious issues, that prompts them. I don't know where you, reader, are at at this point in time. I don't know whether you are still wondering about the existence of God, whether you are actively seeking, or whether you have found and are now serving the One who is King and Lord of All. If you are seeking, then I encourage you to keep doing so. If you know and serve the Christ whom we seek to elevate and commend through this book, then I pray that you will continue to serve him in the Church and in the world with zeal and with faithfulness.

I hope all of you can hear my plea for the Church to be involved in God's wider world. I hope all have got a sense that I feel there is no incongruity for Christian ministers to be involved in the world of sport. I hope that you have a greater understanding of what sports chaplains do, showing the reality of their Christian faith by deeds and, as appropriate, by words.

Sometimes, in those emergencies of life which affect us all, people come to think more deeply about spiritual matters, about eternity, about God. Yet, the truth is that we don't have to wait until there is some crisis or some emergency. The importance and relevance of the person and message of Jesus Christ is for all and every situation, the famous and the unknown, the rich and the poor, the talented and the less gifted. Jesus message is about love and justice, mercy and forgiveness, power to transform life for now and for eternity. It is a message that offers us the certain hope of God's love in our lives now and forever – even beyond life's final whistle.

Postscript

In conclusion, I would like to summarise the work of SCORE. SCORE began in 1991 under the guidance and direction of leaders of the Baptist Union of Great Britain (BUGB). It continues to rely much on the financial support of BUGB, but SCORE is an interdenominational charity, supporting chaplains from many churches in a variety of sports in different ways. This ministry has extended from professional football to non-league football, Rugby League, Rugby Union, golf, county and club cricket, athletics, and, more recently, to the horse-racing world. In 2000 SCORE has extend its work and ministry, with Revd Graham Locking pioneering chaplaincy to the horse-racing world based at Newmarket, and the addition of a new full-time member of staff, Revd Andrew Cowley, operating as Director of Development. There are some other part-time members of staff, but we are mainly a volunteer ministry. Those who serve as chaplains to their local sports clubs or institutions are, by and large, local church ministers. With the support of their local church or congregation, they are typically involved in the local club for between half a day and a day and a half each week. We train, equip, support and resource them in whatever ways we can.

SCORE seeks the support, both prayerful and financial, of those in sympathy with our work and mission. SCORE is affirmed and supported by key Christian leaders from across the United Kingdom. We have never particularly sought to publicise our work and ministry in the media, because the function of chaplaincy is to be more 'servant-hearted' than 'headline grabbing'. Yet we do know that the ministry needs resourcing, and our request for your prayerful and financial support is genuine. All the funds raised by this book are being put back into the charity. We thank you, therefore, for buying *Beyond the Final Whistle*, and hope that in other ways you may be able to further the work and ministry of SCORE. Some basic information about SCORE:

1. Our vision and mission
- To initiate, nurture, support and resource quality chaplaincy to the world of sport.
- To envision and train local churches and their leaders for effective sports ministry within their communities.

Outworking
- To utilise the pastoral training and experience of suitable local church clergy, and then to supplement and enhance it, so that they may become a resource to the sports world via chaplaincy.
- To explain to the world of sport the relevance and benefits of quality sports chaplaincy and to make available to it

SCORE's specialist knowledge and experience.

- To mobilise the Church – both individual clergy and local congregations – to the significance and potential of sports ministry.
- To establish and equip sports chaplains to serve particular clubs, institutions and sports via effective and 'ongoing' chaplaincy involvement.
- To provide expert 'one-off' chaplaincy services to major national and international sports events, as appropriate.
- To establish a UK-wide network of regional support groups dedicated to the training and equipping of chaplains and others involved in SCORE's work and mission.
- To make SCORE known and available throughout the UK as an interdenominational Christian mission with its unique dual focus.
- To open sport across the UK to the chaplaincy concept, so that chaplaincy becomes as accepted and valued in the sports world as it is in the worlds of education, industry, prisons, hospitals or the armed forces.

2. Our service and structure

What SCORE provides

- We believe we offer a unique, specialised and experienced sports chaplaincy service to the UK sports world.
- We provide resources and training for existing sports chaplains through personal support meetings, regional training gatherings and national conferences.
- We seek to identify potential opportunities for chaplaincy services with sport at all levels.
- We are available to work on behalf of sports clubs and

administrators to identify, train and induct potential chaplains.

- We provide quality chaplaincy through experienced and trained personnel to national and international sports events, as well as to local clubs.
- We are training pioneer chaplains to specialise in particular sports.
- We provide resourcing and envisioning workshops for local churches, enabling them to incorporate sport into their local area ministry and community mission programmes.
- We partner, with other organisations of integrity, to provide services to sports bodies across the UK – and, occasionally, beyond.

How SCORE is structured

Our aim is to utilise the training, experience and availability of suitable local clergy to serve sport through chaplaincy. Our structures enable a minimum core staff to co-ordinate and resource local volunteers to serve sport across the UK. The proposed structure below incorporates the appointment of a Director of Development – from April 2000 onwards.

3. Our personnel

Board of Reference

This is a group of people, representing the Church or the sports world, who know of SCORE and are willing to affirm and endorse its ministry.

Revd David Coffey BA General Secretary, Baptist Union of Great Britain

Mr Kenneth Merrett	Secretary, Manchester United Football Club
Mr John Motson	BBC broadcaster and sports commentator
Mr Graham Taylor	Football manager
Revd Dr Derek Tidball BA, BD	Principal, London Bible College
Revd Alan West	Former footballer, now Christian minister

Management committee

These are, in effect, the trustees of SCORE. They have ultimate responsibility for the charity, are elected at the Annual General Meeting, and are answerable to the UK Charity Commissioners, to whom they submit annual reports. Currently, at the time of writing, the management committee consists of:

Mr John Newman FCIS, FIPD	Treasurer, Baptist Union of Great Britain
Revd Ian Marr MA, BD	Co-ordinator, Perth and District YMCA
Mr Brian Waterson FCA	Retired accountant
Mr Brian Smith BSc, ACIB	Service manager, investment banking
Mr Brian Jones FRICS	Retired investment manager
Mr Martin Roach BSc, C Eng, MICE	Civil engineer
Revd David Jeans M Phil, MA, Dip HE	College principal

| Revd David Campbell BA, BD | General Secretary, Bible Society in Northern Ireland |
| Revd Chris Nelson MA, B Th | Clergyman, Chaplain to Preston North End Football Club |

4. Should you wish to learn more about us, please contact us at SCORE at one of the following addresses:

National Headquarters:
SCORE
PO Box 123
Sale
Manchester
M33 4ZA

SCORE in Scotland
PO Box 123
Perth
PH1 1WE

SCORE in Northern Ireland
PO Box 123
Newtownards
BT23 7HG

SCORE in England and Wales
PO Box 123
Watford
Hertfordshire
WD1 7QZ

5. Sports club chaplaincy

The role of a sports club chaplain is:

- **an honorary post, not a paid position**
  Thus the chaplain is free to serve management and staff alike from a neutral position, rather than being seen as an extension of any 'management hierarchy'.
- **a real job, not just a title**
  It involves genuine commitment with regular visits to the club and its staff, plus an 'on call' availability.
- **best done by the most appropriate clergy person**
  Reasonable proximity is helpful, but suitability for the job is more important.
- **best developed when one minister works with those of all denominations**
  The chaplain represents the wider Church, and works with people of all faiths as well as those with no church link at all.

A chaplain is *not*

1. a confrontational preacher, whom people find threatening;
2. a football fanatic living out his or her fantasy or sporting ambition as a chaplain;
3. seeking kudos or benefits – such as free tickets! – through his or her position;
4. a publicity-seeking, self-promoting individual;
5. interested in status, rather than function and service;
6. only active on 'first-team match days';
7. a witch doctor, praying for success.

The clergy person chosen needs to be
1. pastorally gifted;
2. able to make non-church people feel at ease in his or her presence;
3. skilled at interpersonal relationships;
4. willing to represent the wider Church to the club and to other chaplains;
5. able to understand the roles and responsibilities of chaplaincy;
6. free to give sufficient time to the role;
7. servant-hearted, available and flexible;
8. willing to serve the whole club – players and non-players alike;
9. full of integrity, totally confidential and absolutely trustworthy.

SCORE is available to help

by providing clubs with more information or identifying suitable clergy to approach. SCORE organises local, regional and national chaplaincy gatherings to resource, train and encourage existing and potential sports chaplains.

SCORE is happy to make its employees and representatives available to speak about our work, to encourage the development of quality chaplaincy in sport, and to nurture fruitful sports ministry in local churches. All enquiries should be directed to our National Headquarters, preferably by letter.

6. Local church sports ministry

SCORE, and its representatives, very much want to endorse and encourage local church sports ministry. We believe there are many opportunities available to local churches through involvement in the world of sport.

Our National Director, and other representatives, are happy to visit local churches, usually over a long weekend. They can lead a seminar on sport, mission and ministry, speak on behalf of the church at meetings geared for those currently outside the life of the church, and they can take appropriate services on Sundays.

We particularly want to show local churches that there is much more to sports ministry than bringing in a Christian superstar to share their story for fifteen minutes during a service. We very much want to show local churches how, at an ordinary, local grassroots level, sport can be a very effective and relevant medium for the ministry and mission programmes of the local church.

For further details of such weekend visits we ask churches to contact our National Director, in writing, at our national headquarters in Sale, Manchester.

7. Your prayers for us

We invite the prayers and support of Christians of all denominations, and would willingly add your name to our news and prayer letter mailing list if you wish us to do so.

Please write to us at our National Headquarters in Sale, Manchester, and we will ensure that you are mailed three or four times a year with 'SCOREsheet', our news and prayer letter. In the meantime, please pray for us, for all chaplains to the world of sport, and for all who are encouraging effective and fruitful sports ministry in our generation.